EASY WAYS WITH

Flower Arranging

EASY WAYS
WITH

Flower Arranging

Stylish flower displays
in minutes

CORAL WALKER
JANE FORSTER

TIGER BOOKS INTERNATIONAL
LONDON

For Hannah, Alexander, Morgan and Sarah

This edition published in 1995 by
Tiger Books International PLC, Twickenham

First published in Great Britain in 1994 by Anaya Publishers Ltd
London House, Great Eastern Wharf,
Parkgate Road, London SW11 4NQ

Editor	Louisa Somerville
Art Director	Jane Forster
Photography	Shona Wood
Design Assistant	Sarah Willis
Floral designs	Coral Walker and Jane Forster
Painted backgrounds	Kathy Fillion Ritchie

1   3   5   7   9   8   6   4   2

British Library Cataloguing in Publication Data

Walker, Coral
Easy Ways with Flower Arranging: Stylish Flower Displays in
Minutes. – (Easy Ways Series)
I. Title II. Forster, Jane III. Series 745.92

ISBN 1-85501-680-X

Typeset in Great Britain by Art Photoset Ltd, Beaconsfield
Colour reproduction by Typongraph s.r.l., Verona, Italy
Printed and bound in Hong Kong

Contents

Introduction

Arranging flowers has always been a popular pastime, but in recent years it has undergone something of a transformation. No longer the domain of the spinster aunt, flower arranging has become accessible to everyone – still as a satisfying hobby, but also as a valuable tool for interior design and home decoration.

In *Easy Ways with Flower Arranging*, we have approached the subject from a new and refreshing perspective, while still retaining many of the traditional hints and guidelines which have made it such a popular leisure pursuit in the past.

So while many of the designs are free of restraint, nearly all adhere to basic design principles such as balance, colour, form and harmony. And if that sounds technical – it's not, as you'll quickly discover when turning the pages!

There are 35 projects to inspire you – all lavishly illustrated and clearly explained. There's also a host of other ideas to whet your appetite.

The projects are divided into five chapters; each chapter explores different ways of presenting flowers and reveals their wonderful versatility.

Focus on Style and Colour looks at schemes in the home and suggests ways to coordinate flower arrangements with soft furnishings, containers or room settings.

In Table Decorations, there are arrangements for every kind of dining experience, from romantic dinners and summer buffets to harvest suppers and afternoon tea.

Simple Into Special is exactly that, transforming the everyday bunch into something a little more.

For real pizazz, turn to Pushing the Limits – a chapter of lavish and sumptuous floral displays. Yet each arrangement can be accomplished swiftly, easily and practically.

And Last Minute Ideas has a catalogue of clever and novel displays to brighten up a corner of the home, to give as gifts or to decorate the table.

All the flowers are listed by their common names. However, the Latin botanical names for every type of flower appear in the index at the back of the book. The easy-to-access chart on page 114 also lists the botanical names of the most popular plants. For American readers, a US/UK glossary of useful terms appears on page 117.

In *Easy Ways with Flower Arranging*, we have endeavoured to show you how you can create a range of exciting, spectacular or just unusual designs; to make flowers *really* work in your home or for that very special occasion.

FOCUS
ON STYLE
&
COLOUR

*Flowers have become the bright
new tools of interior design – which
means they can be mixed,
matched, and displayed in all sorts
of novel and exciting ways.
This chapter explores a variety of
ideas for using flowers to enhance
your decor, to create a mood or
fashion statement and looks at
flowers from a new perspective.
Take everyday flowers such as
tulips, and employ them as
striking, colour coordinators. Mix
exotic flowers with houseplants for
a tropical look straight from the
brush of Gauguin, or create a
luxurious bathroom display with
lilies and shells.*

Bright and beautiful

Make a play with bold vivid colours like strong primaries or brilliant greens, turquoises or purples. Tulips – in their wide range of colours and with their firm outlines – make the perfect accompaniment to modern settings, vibrant colour schemes and exotic Mexican or Indian-style furnishings and fabrics.

TULIPS
BRIGHTLY COLOURED JUG

Absolutely dead easy! By their very nature, tulips need little in the way of arranging. Once in place, the stems and leaves will curve and drape prettily, creating a wonderful sense of movement.

Trim the ends of the stems to ensure the flowers receive maximum water. Then strip off the bedraggled lower leaves which tend to clog up the neck of the container.

With the red tulips, the flowers have been arranged to create a definite asymmetrical shape. A tight cluster of blooms to one side of the jug is balanced by longer stems fanning out to the right above the handle.

Make the most of double tulips, like these lemon ones, which have pretty pointed leaves. Keep the flowers more or less the same length and tightly pack them into the neck of the jug so that they sit upright.

Tulips will open swiftly once in the home, so put them in shallow water at first and keep them away from radiators, draughts or strong sunlight. To prevent them from drooping excessively, add some carbonated water like soda water to the container. Wrapping them in stiff paper for a couple of hours before arranging them will also help.

VARIATIONS
Great as bold, modern trendsetters, tulips are very versatile and can offset almost any decor. Pastel pinks, white or lilac coloured varieties look absolutely enchanting in a cut crystal, white or pastel jug set at a window against lacy nets or fine Venetian blinds. Or choose richly coloured frilly, Parrot tulips for a Dutch Masters display against heavy velvet drapes in deep red or burgundy.

Create an asymmetrical outline for a little more interest. Make a tight cluster of flowers above the lip and to the front of the jug. Add longer stems to the right hand side, so that they curve out above the handle.

Tulip leaves form a vital part of the display. If you want the leaves to curl away from the stem, gently stroke them between your finger and thumb. Don't be too vigorous or the leaf will split.

Sparkling emerald curtains provide the perfect foil for acid lemon tulips in a green glass jug. Deep scarlet tulips were chosen to offset a medley of yellows and golds.

I v o r y s i l k

Make bathtime a totally luxurious experience. These fabulous Casablanca lilies, with their opulent shapes and exotic stamens are pure lasciviousness! Combine them with creamy-coloured alstroemeria for a wonderful display which takes just minutes to arrange.

This arrangement is set on an Edwardian washstand, but it would look just as well on a shelf or wide windowsill against pretty frosted glass.

WHITE LILIES
CREAM ALSTROEMERIA
FLORAL FOAM
OVAL PLATE

Alstroemeria, also known as the Peruvian lily, is not a true lily, but has lily or azalea-shaped flowers. Because of their complementary shape, they make the perfect foil for the larger lilies.

Any large white lilies work well. These Casablanca lilies are expensive to buy but last for up to two weeks and can be used in a larger display first. Once the flowers at the top of the stems are fading, snip off the flowers lower down to create your bathtime piece.

Begin by preparing the base of the display. Use two small circular tablets of floral foam and soak them well before placing them on to an oval dinner plate. Depending upon the size of the plate, you may only need one circular piece of foam and one semi circle – if this fits more comfortably on the plate. Keep the foam to the centre of the plate, otherwise it may show through your display.

Exquisite Casablanca lilies with their textured ivory petals and chocolate-coloured stamens sit amidst a cloud of creamy alstromeria. Echo the ivory colours with large shells and other bathroom paraphernalia. This display is guaranteed to make bathtime pure luxury!

Build up a low outline of alstroemeria, to form a gentle wave. Keep the first few stems quite long and insert them, as shown below, at the front, towards one side. The alstroemeria should overlap the plate by at least 5cm (2in). Once this is established, build up this section. Don't let the piece become too high though; about 12cm (5in) above the plate is probably sufficient.

Continue to build the outline with the alstroemeria, filling in with more blooms and leaving a gap in the centre, towards the front, for the lilies.

Although some flower arrangers are in favour of snipping off lily stamens, it would completely spoil this piece. Look again – the stamens are absolutely vital to the drama and beauty of this display. Just take care not to brush against them in your best clothes; the pollen is indelible.

There are three lily flowers here and a bud or two; the stems need to be short. Hold the foam steady as you push the lilies in, or you could be in danger of the whole display sliding off the plate.

A few shells, set at the perimeter of the display, really complete the picture.

Thoroughly soak the foam tablet and place it towards the centre of the plate. Work first on building the outline: insert longish stems of alstroemeria, parallel to the plate.

Now for the pièce de resistance. Push in the lilies one at a time, holding the foam steady as necessary. Use one or two lily buds as well as full flowers.

Continue to form clusters of alstroemeria, covering the foam and filling the plate. Leave a gap towards the front, at the centre, for the lily flowerheads.

VARIATION
Although this vanilla colour scheme will suit all bathrooms, there's no reason why you shouldn't try for a different effect. Deep yellow alstroemeria with bright orange lilies creates a more cheerful display, while dark magenta alstroemeria makes a good foil for wine-coloured Turk's cap lilies – great when styling against claret colours.

Topiary trees

Brighten up a mantelpiece or lone shelf with a couple of cheerful little trees made from colourful dried strawflowers.

These trees can be rustled up during an afternoon and will last a year or two if kept out of strong sunlight.

STRAWFLOWERS
WHITE STATICE
BUTCHER'S BROOM LEAVES
MOSS
SMALL BRANCH
FLORAL WIRE
DRY FLORAL FOAM SPHERE
DRY FLORAL FOAM OFFCUTS
TERRACOTTA POT(S)
GILT WAX

The beauty of these little trees is that they use only two types of dried flowers, both of which are inexpensive to buy or easy to grow and dry yourself.

You can make the trees any size you wish, but smaller ones are quicker to put together and use less material: you might be surprised quite how many flowers it takes to cover even a small foam sphere!

The largest tree here measures about 38cm (15in) high, and fits neatly on to a bookcase or mantelshelf.

Begin by creating the basic tree shape. This is easy.

Take a small branch to form the trunk. Look for old prunings or bits of dead branch when trying to find a suitable trunk. A serrated bread knife will cut most branches of this thickness to length, although a hack saw is probably more professional. Push the foam sphere firmly on to the trunk.

Wedge pieces of foam into the flower pot, (offcuts are fine for this). Push the tree into the pot.

You'll probably need to manoeuvre the tree a little at this stage to establish the correct height. If the tree looks too tall or too short, pull the sphere up a bit or push it further down until you're satisfied with the height.

Strawflowers – also known as everlasting or *immortelle* – make wonderful dried flowers. However, their stems are weak and most that you buy are wire-supported. If you are growing and drying your own they are easy to strengthen yourself. Strawflowers are quite robust and are quickly wired up using the hairpin method – see the step in Tips and Techniques on page 110. Insert the wired flowerheads into the sphere, turning the tree as you work, to get a good balance of colour and a nice rounded shape.

Cheerful strawflowers are the dried flower arranger's delight. Inexpensive, plentiful, easy-to-grow and dry, they are the perfect solution for these jolly little trees which will last for well over a year.

Don't cram the flowerheads together too tightly, as you'll need to slot in little clusters of statice. Bind these with sticky tape to make a stronger 'stem'.

At this stage you can give your trees slightly different features – if you are making more than one.

Here, the larger tree has a little frill of statice around the base of the sphere, to cover the top of the trunk. Butcher's broom leaves are then interspersed throughout the tree to break up the density of colour.

On the smaller tree, this isn't necessary, and the leaves form the frill around the base of the sphere instead.

To finish off both trees, tuck a little moss around the trunk at the base to cover the foam. Give the pots a touch of artists' gilt wax if you wish.

Little topiary trees enliven a dull shelf or enhance a simple mantelpiece. Made from just two varieties of dried flowers, they are inexpensive to assemble, yet the finished result is both attractive and professional.

Fill the pot with offcuts of dry foam, wedging them in tightly to give the trunk support. Push the sphere on to the trunk and insert the whole tree into the pot.

Fill out the sphere with wired strawflowers, mixing the colours to achieve a good balance. Even on a small sphere you'll need a lot of flowerheads; don't underestimate the amount.

Tuck in small sprays of butcher's broom around the base of the smaller sphere to form a little frill. Take care when using this plant as the leaves have deceptively sharp spines.

Disguise the foam with a little carpet of moss. Gilt wax dabbed around the rim of the pot adds a classic touch. This useful substance can be found in art shops or picture framing stores.

Gentleman's study

Flowers are rarely associated with any masculine domain; yet this subtle arrangement is thoroughly at home with the polished wood and heavy drapes of the billiard room or gentleman's study.

For this more masculine piece, use old pewter tankards as containers. Fill them with sprigs of plush, burgundy-coloured foliage, a few love-in-a-mist seedheads and a bunch of pale mauve scabious or pincushion flowers.

The effect is classic!

LILAC COLOURED SCABIOUS
COPPER-COLOURED FOLIAGE
LOVE-IN-A-MIST SEEDHEADS
PEWTER TANKARDS

Old pewter, with its lovely dull, gunmetal sheen, looks beautiful on richly-polished wood. It is this combination which has inspired this display.

If you don't want to put your flowers straight into the tankard, pop another container inside. The bottom of a plastic bottle is ideal.

Begin by filling the tankard with sprays of foliage – smoketree (*Cotinus*) was used here, but you can use any copper foliage. Strip and hammer the stem ends well.

For the best effect, make sure the foliage is at least twice the height of the container, so that the final arrangement is well balanced.

Once the foliage is in place, slot in stems of scabious. Vary the length of the stems to create an even effect throughout. The pale mauve petals instantly light up the display.

Finally, tuck in stems of love-in-a-mist seedheads. These are all the better if they are on the verge of drying out as they will still bear their feathery foliage. The little lines on the seedheads are a warm burgundy colour – the perfect companion to the foliage.

Mauve-coloured scabious combine with coppery smoke tree foliage and love-in-a-mist seedheads. The mixture of colours and textures evokes a more masculine image, especially when set in pewter on highly polished wood.

Fill the tankard with water and begin forming the outline with sprays of the coppery foliage. Condition the stems well, so that they can drink easily and don't wither prematurely.

Insert stems of scabious among the foliage. Cut the stems to varying heights to create a really full shape. See how the pale mauve instantly brightens the display, offsetting both the foliage and the pewter.

Gauguin

Capture the exotic in your conservatory or living room by mixing houseplants with a few brilliantly-coloured blooms. The look is 'jungle' or even 'paradise' and could be straight from the paintings of Gauguin or Henri Rousseau.

Fill a wall or corner of the room with this lavish arrangement. Stack the plants at different heights for the best effect and replace the flowers as they die to make this a really long-lasting display.

MIXED HOUSEPLANTS
BIRDS OF PARADISE
ORANGE OR DEEP CORAL GLADIOLI
LIZZIEANTHUS
STARGAZER LILIES
OLD WINE AND BEER BOTTLES
PLANT TROUGH OR
PLANK OF WOOD AND BRICKS

Fun and flamboyant: this arrangement makes the most of unusual plants and flowers, without spending an absolute fortune.

The more houseplants you have, the bigger your display. However, even with say, five or six plants of different sizes, you can achieve a spectacular effect.

First assemble your houseplants – a mixture looks best. Although variegated plants look good in this arrangement; ones with coloured leaves – like the Joseph's coat plants (*Codiaeum*) – do not. Remember that bushy, tall plants will give the most cover and look the most lush. It's also worth avoiding deliberately trailing plants, such as ivy, as these detract from the line and shape you are trying to establish.

Mix leafy potted plants with bold and flamboyant flowers to recreate a tropical paradise. Use leafy houseplants and a selection of brightly-coloured blooms like birds of paradise, which look absolutely spectacular with their bold orange and purple heads.

A guide to some of the more popular houseplants which are successful in this display appears opposite.

For the best effect, place your houseplants at different levels: keep the largest and tallest plants to the back or on the floor.

Begin by creating a tier close to the wall. You could use a plant trough or a small plank of wood balanced on two piles of bricks.

Place a few plants on the tier and some of the larger ones in the foreground on the floor. You can even upend an old flowerpot and stand a plant on it to achieve a layered effect. As well as height, remember to create some depth away from the wall by using plants in old terracotta or stone pots towards the front, as the bases of these will be visible. (Don't spoil everything by allowing the foreground plants to be seen in plastic flowerpots!)

At this stage, leave some gaps and reserve at least one largish plant and two or three small ones for filling in.

Bring together your flowers and bottles. Fill the bottles with water. Now trim off all the stem ends so the plants can drink easily. Put the birds of paradise in position first, arranging their 'beaks' so that they point out in different directions. As their stems are so thick, you will probably squeeze only one or two into one bottle.

Next position some of the background flowers like the gladioli and lizzieanthus. Clumps of colour are effective, so instead of scattering the rich purple lizzieanthus, keep them in a group towards the back.

Split the stems of gladioli into several bottles to create varying levels and spots of warm colour.

Save the Stargazer lilies to the end and make these your focal point. If they don't all fit into one bottle, use two bottles and stand them close together.

With the flowers more or less in position, stand back and assess the display. Any gaps should now be apparent. Take the remaining houseplants and slot them in to conceal any visible plastic pots, noticeable bottles or obvious holes. Now is also the time to add in the larger houseplant you put to one side earlier. It's uncanny how this final plant will complete the scene.

Fill old, clean wine and beer bottles with water. Insert one or more flowers into each bottle (bear in mind that birds of paradise stems are very thick). They are now ready to be inserted into the houseplant jungle.

Exotic birds of paradise combine with bright pink Stargazer lilies and lustrous houseplants as part of an extraordinary indoor tropical paradise.

HINT
If you have a limited number of good-sized houseplants, use pots of cut shrubbery or shiny foliage to camouflage the bottles bearing the flowers. Or add to your existing plant collection with potted ferns or palms which are quite inexpensive to buy if the specimens are small. These are useful to tuck into unsightly gaps.

Popular houseplants to use
Bird's nest fern (*Asplenium nidus avis*)
Calathea sp.
Castor-oil plant (*Ricinus communis*)
Dumb cane (*Dieffenbachia* sp.)
Ferns (*Nephrolepis*)
Fiddle leaf fig (*Ficus lyrata*)
Parlour palm (*Neanthe bella*)
Philodendron
Peace lily (*Spathiphyllum* 'Mauna Loa')
Swiss cheese plant (*Monstera deliciosa*)
Rubber plant (*Ficus robusta*)
Silhouette plant (*Dracaena marginata*)
Tropical palm (*Phoenix*)
Weeping fig (*Ficus benjamina*)

Something Moorish

An exotic tiled panel in cobalt blue, white and deep yellow, is the inspiration for this traditional arrangement. The colours in the tiles have been picked up by a variety of blooms: deep blue monkshood, golden yellow chrysanthemums and white freesias and tulips. The swirling patterns in the tiles are echoed in the golden rod and hebe.

MONKSHOOD
CHRYSANTHEMUMS
HEBE
WHITE FREESIAS
WHITE TULIPS
GOLDEN ROD
BLUE GLASS BOWL
FLORAL FOAM
WIRE MESH

This classical display is built up in a triangular shape. It's quite important to construct it in a container with a stem so that you can achieve a really majestic effect. Use a fruit bowl, cakestand or large glass dessert dish, for example.

Fill your bowl with soaked floral foam. Take a piece of wire mesh and stretch this across the top of the bowl.

Start with the outline flowers: the fabulously curving stems of golden rod and hebe. Establish the height at the back of the display, and bring the flowers down through both sides and towards the front in a crescent shape. Allow the flowers at the front to drape forwards over the edge.

In the centre, towards the back of the display, insert tall stems of monkshood. These vivid purple flowers are related to delphinium, and it's easy to see why. Their plush velvety flowers are shaped like small helmets or hoods – hence the name.

With the monkshood in place, take the chrysanthemums, placing taller stems

An elaborate tiled panel, reminiscent of the ancient Spanish or Moorish civilisations, is the inspiration for this traditional display. Cobalt blue, rich yellow, brown and white have all been emulated with a careful selection of flowers.

towards the back and bringing shorter ones into the centre to form the focal point. Their lovely little button faces of yellow and brown are a perfect match for the tile pattern.

Now add the white highlights provided by the tulips and freesias. As the tulips curve so gracefully, keep these to the sides of the display, to follow the line established by the golden rod and hebe. Insert the freesias towards the front of the bowl.

Build up the outline with curving stems of golden rod and hebe. Take the display out as wide as you can, but don't let it grow too tall as the balance will be wrong.

Use the golden rod and hebe to curve towards the front to form a crescent shape. Slot in the purple monkshood towards the back to establish the height.

Insert the chrysanthemums. Place taller stems to the back and come down through the front with shorter sprays. Make these the focal point, turning their faces towards you.

Complete the arrangement with highlights of white tulips and long stems of freesias. The tulips follow the curving shape of the outline, while the freesias complement the foreground.

Winter solstice

This mantlepiece, with its gilt mirror and carved white surround, is the inspiration for a winter arrangement. Golden cord, bronzed hydrangea heads and creamy white lilies, are set against a glossy swag of evergreen laurel leaves. The whole display is then illuminated with tiny points of white light.

WHITE LILIES
SHINY EVERGREEN LEAVES SUCH AS LAUREL
DRIED MOP-HEAD HYDRANGEAS
IVY FLOWERS
POPPY SEEDHEADS
GOLD SPRAY PAINT
GOLD CORD
FLORAL FOAM
FLORAL ADHESIVE TAPE
WIRE
STICKY FIXERS
STRING OF FAIRY LIGHTS
HEAVY-DUTY STICKY TAPE
CRIMSON RIBBON

Whether for Christmas or just to cheer a winter gathering, this sumptuous swag adds a note of splendour to any occasion.

As the complete swag weighs very little, it can be suspended with just a little tape and some sticky fixers.

First, make sure the lights reach the shelf when plugged in and that the trailing wire can be discreetly taped out of sight. If not, you might need to lengthen the wire or use an extension lead.

About 2 metres (2 yards) of cord should fit most shelves. Tape the cord to one end of the shelf, using heavy-duty sticky tape. Bring the cord along the front of the shelf, draping it gently. Secure it to the centre point with sticky fixers. Drape the cord along the remainder of the shelf and tape it at the other end.

Now run the fairy lights along the cord, attaching the flex to the cord at various intervals with little twists of wire.

Cut a brick of fresh floral foam in half and soak both pieces thoroughly. Using the floral adhesive tape, secure these two pieces to the shelf; one at the end, the other towards the centre at the opposite end. It's quite important to tape the foam down, as the whole thing will topple forwards if it's not firmly in place.

Once the basic structure is in position, you can begin to add the foliage. Use slender stems, these are more pliable. If you can, twist the foliage in and out of the cord, securing it at intervals with pieces of wire. Make sure that the flex of the lights is covered as much as possible, but that the light bulbs are visible.

Before you tackle each floral cluster, you'll need to spray some of the hydrangea heads and all the poppy seedheads with gold paint.

Glossy green laurel leaves form the basis for this winter-time swag. Offset with clusters of white lilies and frosted hydrangea heads, the whole arrangement is illuminated with tiny Christmas lights.

Intertwine slender stems of evergreen foliage along the cord, attaching them at intervals with little twists of wire. Stand back to assess the size of the swag. It should be leafy but not so dense it loses definition.

Cut the stems of the lilies quite short and insert them into the foam. If the foam begins to pull forward with the weight of the flowers, push a small apple wedged on to a cocktail stick into the back of the foam.

Use the gold-sprayed poppy seedheads to add depth to the flower cluster. Allow a few to protrude out over the draping lilies and buds.

Begin with the clusters of hydrangea heads. Use a mixture of gold and naturally-dried red flowers. Fix some at both ends of the shelf and a few towards the centre, as shown. Where you have floral foam in position, slot the hydrangea stems into this. At the end where there is no foam, stick the stems of the hydrangeas to the shelf with a few sticky fixers.

At this stage, intertwine a length of

Drape a mantelpiece with boughs of shiny laurel and thread through tiny fairy lights. Adorned with creamy lilies and frosted hydrangea heads, you have a spectacular winter display.

crimson ribbon, trailing it from the left hand side of the swag, through to the centre. Ribbon with fine wire along its outer edges is best as it holds its shape.

With the hydrangeas in place, you can add the lilies to each of the foam bricks. Cut the stems quite short, and fan the flowers out, allowing some to hang down. Use buds as well as open blooms.

Remember to make the flower cluster towards the centre of the swag more dominant than the one at the end. Fill out the larger cluster with a few stems of laurel.

In among the lilies tuck the gold-sprayed poppy seedheads. Push some well in to create a feeling of depth.

The sphere-shaped flowers of the ivy are a wonderful wintertime sight and just three or four will enhance the display.

Switch on the fairy lights and adjust any that have become hidden.

DECORATIONS FOR TABLES

This is where flowers really come into their own. No special dinner, buffet or garden party would be complete without a flower display. But cast out any preconceptions and take a fresh approach to table decorations.

Use swathes of ivy and Russian vine to trail around ivory-coloured candles and night lights, float chrysanthemum heads in shallow glass dishes and illuminate them with dancing candlelight, or garland a platter of bright red summer fruits with brilliant scarlet geranium heads and sweet peas for that special garden party.

Summer's evening

Lofty cream candles are wreathed with ivy and lacy Russian vine then trimmed with fat bunches of green grapes. Set this stylish arrangement in the garden for a sophisticated summer's evening party.

IVY
RUSSIAN VINE
GREEN GRAPES
CREAM SATIN RIBBON
LOW CANDELABRA
CREAM CANDLES

Cut long stems of trailing ivy and Russian vine and shake it well to ensure that it's free from insects. It's also a good idea to rinse the ivy; this cleans off any nasties and gives the leaves a glossy shine.

First, wind the ivy round the candelabra. If you don't have one, use four low candlesticks instead and lay the ivy around them, and on to the table. Allow the ivy to trail across the table.

With the ivy in position, you can start intertwining the Russian vine. The delicate, frothy flowers of this plant complement the deep green ivy.

Allow plenty of ribbon, preferably in one long length. Around 2–3m (2–3yd) of ribbon is ideal so you can incorporate plenty of curls and twists. Wind the ribbon in and out of the plants and around the candelabra. Let this, too, trail across the table for a flowing sense of movement.

For the finishing touch, add a bunch of green grapes to the centre of the display.

VARIATION
Vary this idea slightly for a dinner party. Make the display here for the centrepiece and twist a little Russian vine around each napkin at the place settings.

To complete each place setting, put a nightlight on a small saucer and wind a little ivy and vine round the edge.

For a balmy summer's evening buffet add style and elegance to the outdoors with ivory-coloured candles swathed in ivy and frothy Russian vine. Intertwine lengths of satin cream ribbon and complete the display with bunches of plump green grapes.

Nordic lights

Foliage preserved with glycerine takes on the warm, burnished glow of beaten bronze. For leaves like those of fern or bracken, this treatment displays their intricate leaves to the best advantage. Set these spectacular fronds against magnolia-coloured silk and intersperse them with autumn yellow chrysanthemums and tiny nightlights.

PRESERVED BRACKEN/FERN
YELLOW DAISY CHRYSANTHEMUMS
NIGHTLIGHTS
GLASS NIGHTLIGHT HOLDERS
SMALL SAUCERS
FLORAL FOAM
SILK FABRIC

Invest in a little silk fabric – about 1m (1yd) will more than suffice – as this will be your background. The silk can then be placed over a plain tablecloth or directly on to a polished wood table.

Allow the silk to move and form little waves as you lay it down.

You can buy preserved fern quite easily, especially in the autumn when the new season's dried flowers become available. However, it's quite easy to preserve some yourself, see page 113 for details.

Select the best fern specimens, as every frond will be on display.

Lay the ferns in a pattern across the centre of the table. Snip off some of the stems, otherwise they may criss-cross and form too strong a pattern.

Now position the nightlights, in their holders, among the fern fronds.

With the basic pattern arranged, make up two or three little domes of fresh chrysanthemums. Bright yellow or bright orange work well.

To make the domes, put a little piece of wet floral foam on to a small saucer. Cut the stems of the chrysanthemums down to around 4cm (1½in) and insert them into the foam. Start with the flower in the centre and work down the sides.

For a little variety, make one piece asymmetrical, with longer flower stems and buds protruding from one side.

Just before dinner, scatter a few flowerheads on to the table and tuck in a few around a nightlight. These will last without water for the evening.

HINT
Look out for silk remnants in fabric shops; even large silk scarves or wraps at charity shops or rummage sales can work well. As a natural fabric, silk moves in a flowing manner which cheaper, manmade fabrics find difficult to emulate.

Lightly ruffled cream silk provides a backcloth for fabulous fronds of glycerined fern and bright yellow chrysanthemums. The whole display is lit with tiny white nightlights set in small clear glass holders.

Push short stems of chrysanthemums into a piece of well-soaked floral foam set on to a small saucer. For an interesting variation, take longer stems bearing small flowerheads and buds, and push these in down one side. Tuck in a couple of tiny fern fronds among the yellow flowers.

Tea at three

Afternoon tea on the lawn or patio is given a touch of elegance with a pretty coordinating arrangement that can be used later to decorate a windowsill or kitchen dresser.

Choose colours to complement your china. This combination looks splendid against traditional blue and white.

DEEP PURPLE AND PALE MAUVE PETUNIAS
WHITE BUSY LIZZIES (*IMPATIENS*)
PURPLE/WHITE VERBENA
COPPER TROUGH
PLASTIC BAG OR CLING FILM
GRAVEL

Bedding plants are all too frequently neglected when thinking of flower arrangements in the traditional sense. Yet they can be really useful for last minute displays and, if left in their soil, they'll give lasting pleasure.

Old copper looks particularly pretty as a container for bedding plants, but you can use a terracotta or even plastic planter, as long as it's not too big.

As most plant troughs come with drainage holes, you'll need to line your container with cling film, otherwise the moisture and soil could damage your table linen. By lining the trough, you'll prevent the soil from draining properly, so add some gravel to counteract this before putting in the plants.

Water the plants first. The soil should be wet but not soggy. Gently ease the plants from their plastic pots. Do this by squeezing the sides of the pot and tapping it firmly underneath. Hold the plant by the base of the stem and give it a little careful assistance; it should come out with most of the soil intact.

Arrange the plants rather as you would any display, aiming for a good balance of colour, depth and outline. Use the white flowers for highlights and to offset the other colours.

Complete this whole operation on old newspaper. This way any loose soil can be gathered up and used to fill out the trough or put on to the garden.

The soil should be covered automatically by the mass of the leaves once all the plants are in place. However, if you do have any soil showing, disguise it with a little wispy spagnum moss.

A selection of purple and white bedding plants nestle in a glowing copper trough. An unusual but practical teatime arrangement that lasts long after the guests depart.

Line the trough with polythene or cling film to prevent water and soil trickling on to your table linen. Put in a layer of loose gravel before adding the plants; this will help counteract the poor drainage.

Gently squeeze the plants out of their plastic pots and place them on old newspaper. Add them to the trough, pushing the soil down firmly. Aim for a harmonious balance of colour and shape.

Pink crystal

Little ropes of freesias, pinks and anemones meander between garlanded crystal candlesticks for an intimate dinner *à deux*.

This unashamedly romantic table decoration is a combination of sugar pinks and creamy whites with a sweet-scented fragrance.

Because the flowers are out of water, they need to be assembled on the day of the dinner. Keep them well misted with water and wrapped in moist tissue paper until you're ready to position them.

To garland the candlesticks
PINKS
FLORAL TAPE
REEL WIRE
TALL GLASS CANDLESTICKS
DOUBLE-SIDED TAPE

Whatever candleholders you choose, make sure they are long and slim.

Hold a piece of wire up against the candlestick. Allowing for a little extra at the top and bottom, cut the wire with a pair of scissors.

Cut the stems of the pinks to about 5cm (2in) in length. Leave about 4cm (1½in) of wire at the top and hold the first pink tight to the wire. Take the stretchy floral tape and begin binding the stem to the wire. Before the stem is completely covered, cut the tape and secure it by stretching it tightly.

Now take the next flower and lay this against the first, so that the head sits neatly underneath. Bind this flower in the same way to the wire.

Tall crystal glass candlesticks are garlanded with little ropes of garden pinks, while clusters of anemones, hebe and more pinks meander across the table. Pink moiré ribbon curls and twists between the blooms in this table decoration for the truly romantic.

Continue with more flowers until you reach the bottom of the wire. On the last flower make sure the wire and stem are completely covered by tape.

Hook the top of the wire over the rim of the candleholder (it will be hidden by the candle) and twist the flower rope around the stem of the candlestick until you reach the base. Secure the bottom of the rope to the candlestick with a few pieces of double-sided tape.

Flower clusters for the table
PINKS
WHITE FREESIAS
DEEP PINK AND WHITE ANEMONES
WHITE HEBE
FLORAL TAPE
MOIRÉ RIBBON
DOUBLE-SIDED OR MASKING TAPE

The table decoration is made up of several little flower posies, laid out in a gentle wave, linking the two candlesticks. The posy stems are hidden with dusky pink moiré ribbon to give the appearance of a winding rope of flowers.

Gather several stems of flowers together and bind them tightly with floral tape. Make sure you include a little of the pretty anemone foliage, as the leaves give depth and interest. Trim the ends of the posy to neaten any straggling stems.

Once you've made four or five little posies, begin positioning them on the table, gently curving them around the candlesticks. Let the flowerheads of one bunch cover the stem ends of another to give the effect of a continuous rope; although any visible bits of tape can be covered with the ribbon.

Now twist the ribbon along the length of the flowers, covering any gaps as you go. To keep the ribbon in place, stick tiny pieces of double-sided tape at strategic points on the tablecloth, and adhere the ribbon to this. Double-sided tape is easily removed, and shouldn't leave any marks if you pull it gently away.

The colour range of anemones offers an interesting choice. Here, dusky pink and magnolia-tinted petals give these flower clusters a coordinated look.

Tape short stems of pinks along the length of wire, overlapping the flowers as you go. Don't use too much tape or the piece will become bulky and unsightly. Remember to stretch the tape as you bind it (see page 111).

Hook the top of the wire to the rim of the candlestick and curve the flower rope down the stem. Secure the rope at the base with a little double-sided tape. It will be hidden by the flower rope.

Make up little posies of mixed flowers including some of the anemone foliage with its attractively-shaped leaves. Bind the stems with floral tape and trim off the ends with sharp scissors for a neat finish.

With the candlesticks in position, begin placing the little posies in a gentle wave across the table. Try to put the flowerheads of one posy covering the stems ends of another for a continuous effect.

Strawberry fair

Brilliant scarlet flowers ring a platter of red summer fruits. Choose a mix of the brightest blooms around, letting the different shades of red clash fiercely. Redcurrants, watermelon and plump strawberries spill out from one edge.

Selection of bright red flowers
PELARGONIUM (GERANIUM)
POT DIANTHUS
SPRAY CARNATIONS
SWEET PEAS
FUCHSIAS

VINE LEAVES
EUCALYPTUS FOLIAGE
WIRE RING
FLORAL FOAM
PLATTER
RED SUMMER FRUITS

Luscious summer strawberries and jewel-bright redcurrants are piled high with slices of garnet-coloured watermelon. A sumptuous buffet dessert is decorated with scarlet and crimson summer flowers.

Bedding plants like pot dianthus (small carnations) and pelargoniums (more commonly known as geraniums) with their vivid colours are prime for this type of display, yet are frequently overlooked for a fresh flower arrangement. Slotted into wet floral foam, they last well.

Choose an attractive platter, as it will be on show, especially once guests tackle the fruit.

Wire rings are available from floral suppliers; they're inexpensive and come in a range of sizes, so you should be able to match one to your chosen platter.

Sit the ring on to the platter and cut a couple of foam tablets in half and slot

A spectacular platter of red summer fruits and vibrant red flowers create an eye-catching buffet dessert.

Place the wire ring on the platter and slot in sections of well-drenched floral foam. Cut the foam so that it can be wedged tightly into the ring.

Slot in trailing stems of foliage first; these will begin to cover the wire and form a backdrop for the flowers. Among the foliage begin forming clusters of flowers.

When you have completed the outline, add the pretty fuchsia bells at the front. Check the overall balance and readjust any of the other flowers, making sure there are no gaps.

them into the ring, as shown. Make sure the foam is well drenched with water; on a hot day the plants will need all the moisture they can get. Leave one quarter of the ring empty as this is where the fruit will tumble out.

With the ring and foam in position, begin inserting the vine leaves and eucalyptus to form a backdrop. Among the foliage, slot small stems of the various red flowers, keeping them in clusters close together.

Save the fuchsias till last, as these are delicate blooms and will not stand much manoeuvring. Use one of the *Fuchsia magellanica* varieties; these are more slender and a deeper red than the *F fulgens* varieties.

Continue to pack out the ring, tucking in little pieces of foliage to fill in any gaps, but keep the display predominantly bright red.

Add the fuchsias when you are more or less happy with everything else. Tuck a few pieces at the front to fall over the edge of the platter.

Fill the centre with fruit, letting strawberries and redcurrants tumble through the gap at the front.

HINT
Keep the flowers and fruit misted with water if it is a hot day; it will keep everything looking fresh and appetising.

Autumn's fruits

Create a harvest or Thanksgiving table of sumptuous splendour, gathering together the fruits of autumn.

Gourds, fruiting fig, sweetcorn and bunches of little yellow capsicum combine with a mixture of flowers, hops, wheat and barley, but you can use any number of fruits, vegetables and mixed plant material. Let the display tumble and spill over the table in a celebration of plenty.

WHEAT
BLACK-EARED BARLEY
DRIED SUNFLOWERS
FRUITED FIG BRANCHES
CAPSICUM
HOPS
SWEETCORN
GOURDS
NASTURTIUMS
ORANGE BALL DAHLIAS
PLATE
COCKTAIL STICKS
FLORAL FOAM
FLORAL TAPE

Construct this whole display on a dinner plate and two pieces of dry floral foam.

Cut a brick of foam in half. Put one piece on to the dinner plate, the other directly on to the table next to the plate. (You can tape the foam down to give it more stability, but this is not crucial).

Create a flowing shape along the length of the table with stems of the fruited fig. The large leaves help cover the foam and plate as well as providing a backcloth for the rest of the arrangement.

Push two or three cocktail sticks into the gourd to anchor it to the foam. Really tough gourds might need to have the holes bored first. Use wooden skewers if the gourd is particularly tough or heavy.

Tuck in bright orange ball dahlias to complement the rounded shapes of the sunflowers. Keep the dahlias in a group, to one side of the display.

Fruiting stems of fig, with their giant, deeply-lobed leaves create a basic outline and cover most of the foam and plate.

Set among this the heavier gourds and sweetcorn, peeling the husk back to reveal the golden nuggets of corn.

To secure the larger gourds and sweetcorn in place, use two or three cocktail sticks per item, piercing one end into the vegetable and the other into the foam. See the step below for guidance.

Really heavy gourds may need something a little stronger; use wooden skewers instead.

Add in smaller gourds to the centre of the display and build up and out with clusters of short-stemmed dried sunflowers and branches of capsicum.

At this time of the year, you should be able to glean wheat from the fields. Black-eared barley lends variety and echoes the husk of the sweetcorn.

Make up several bunches of wheat and one of barley. Keep the ears level and bind the stems with tape. Trim off the stem ends to give you a neat bunch. Place these throughout the display; taking one short bunch at the back to add substance to taller items.

Use the ball dahlias to fill out the shape, concentrating them in a cluster close to the sunflowers.

Trail stems of green hops across the front of the display, letting them tumble over the edge of the table.

Stand back and make sure there are no awkward gaps or pieces of foam or plate showing through. Tuck in pieces of foliage or wheat to hide anything.

Celebrate harvest or Thanksgiving with a plentiful display of autumn fruits and flowers. Fruiting figs form the backdrop to plump gourds, dried sunflowers, orange nasturtiums and ropes of fresh hops.

Floating flowers

Floating candles send flickering lights and sparkling reflections across the dinner table, creating an atmosphere of warmth.

Set the candles in shallow glass to achieve maximum highlights and combine them with jaunty flowerheads in matching colours.

DAISY CHRYSANTHEMUMS IN TWO COLOURS
FLOATING CANDLES IN THREE COLOURS
WIDE BUT SHALLOW GLASS DISH

Daisy-type flowers are the most successful for floating; they lie flat, with their pretty eyes staring up at you. Chrysanthemums like these come in a good colour range so you should easily match the candles.

It's best to test the candles beforehand, as some makes do not float well. These poorer quality candles are often difficult to light and the wick is quickly embedded in surrounding wax. They also extinguish themselves prematurely, either by taking on board too much water, or by burning through into a hole.

Candles to look for are quite large and are fairly thick in the middle. Floating candles should last about four hours when lit.

Make sure the glass bowl is sparkling clean. Fill it carefully with water. Snip the heads from the chrysanthemums and float them in the water. Mix large and small heads together, leaving gaps between for the candles.

Position the candles carefully or water will wash on to them, wetting the wicks and making them difficult to light.

These pretty dancing lights will captivate dinner guests, yet this table decoration can be thrown together in minutes. Orange, red and yellow give a wonderful warm glow.

For an alternative colourway, try green and blue floating candles with white daisy chrysanthemums. It's a cooler look for a totally different effect.

SIMPLE
INTO
SPECIAL

*What can you do to make that
everyday bouquet or garden bunch
a bit special?
In this chapter, we look at some of
the most popular cut flowers:
carnations, roses and daffodils, to
name a few, and given them a little
imaginative treatment.
Turn your hand to painting
carnations! Or use abundant
spring flowers to create rich carpets
of colour. Take a new look at
garden sticks as part of a flower
display. And create the ultimate in
country-style baskets with a
medley of flowers and plants from
the garden or hedgerow.*

Spring colour

Pack spring garden flowers tightly into shallow glass containers and create a visual feast of fresh, bright colour.

DAFFODILS
BLUEBELLS
WHITE FREESIAS
YELLOW RANUNCULUS
FORGET-ME-NOTS
GLASS BOWLS
CLEAR MARBLES

Plentiful spring flowers like daffodils cheer the heart after winter has passed and early sunshine begins to warm the garden. Make the most of these inexpensive and popular flowers by cramming them tightly into bowls to maximize their fresh colour and lush petals.

Alongside daffodils, use other spring flowers. Crocus look beautiful, but wither too quickly as a cut flower. Instead, use freesias. They have a similar shape and come in the same colour range. They also last well when cut.

If kept quite cool, bluebells can survive as cut flowers, although their time span is relatively short. Select really strong stems and robust flower bells for the best results.

Keep each flower type and colour to one container. As daffodils emit a substance from their stems which can be toxic to other flowers, it's worth keeping them separate anyway.

You will need to keep the stems short, so that the flowerheads just rest on the rim of the bowl. To do this, measure one flower against the bowl before you cut the stem. Use this flower as a guide for cutting the others. When you've cut most of the stems down, gather the flowers together into little groups and stack them into the bowl. This will keep the stems looking neat and achieve a flat top to the display.

In the larger containers, it will help if you add some clear marbles first. These give the stems some necessary support and prevent the flowers from leaning over at an awkward angle.

Once you've filled four or five different sized bowls with flowers, group them together for terrific impact.

Group bright spring colours together in clear glass bowls for a modern, yet classic, arrangement.

Measure one flower up against the side of the container. Cut the stem so that the flowerhead just rests on the rim of the glass. Use this flower as a guide for cutting the others to the right height.

Once you've cut the flowers to the right height, begin to gather them into little groups before pushing them into the marbles. This keeps the stems in a neat formation and the flowerheads level.

Sticks and tricks

Gently waving gerbera are splinted with pea sticks and slotted into modern tube vases. The pea sticks give the flowers some much-needed support and add a zany note to a simple display.

Gerbera are the ultimate in daisies; their other name is Transvaal daisy. With their perfectly-formed heads and sizzling colour range – they are great fun to work with.

Here, advantage has been taken of their volatile stems, which have a tendency to twist rather alarmingly. By tying them with tiny raffia bows to ordinary garden sticks, the flowers are given some support and a contemporary display is achieved at the same time.

The tube-style vases are old postage tubes, painted to match the gerbera.

GERBERA
PEA STICKS
GREEN RAFFIA
POSTAGE TUBE
EMULSION PAINT
CRAFT PLASTER
PVA MEDIUM
TUMBLERS

It's rather satisfying to make your own vases for this type of display. Alternatively, you'll need three similar, cylindrical vases to achieve this effect.

Cut the tube into three 23cm (9in) lengths and paint liberally with PVA. When dry, coat with a craft plaster solution, sprinkling a little dry plaster to the wet surface. Leave this to dry, then coat with emulsion paint. The tubes dry with a lovely rugged texture.

When they're ready, slot one over an ordinary glass tumbler and you have a modern vase. Just take care when moving the two items together that you keep your hand underneath the tube to support the tumbler inside, as these vases have no base!

Begin by tying the gerbera to the sticks. Use tiny pieces of green raffia. Raffia comes in many shades; here, two different greens are used to add interest. Tie the raffia around the pea stick and the stem, about 7cm (3in) below the flowerhead and again about the same distance from the end of the stem.

Assemble the vases in position, as they are difficult to move once you begin.

Add the splinted gerbera to the vases, using two or three shades of one colour or complementary colours.

Lay the gerbera on its side against the pea stick. Take a small length of raffia and tie the pea stick to the stem, about 7cm (3in) from the flowerhead. Tie the gerbera to the stick further down the stem, about the same distance from the end.

With the gerbera secured at both ends, the flowers are easy to arrange.

Country basket

Laden with a medley of late summer colours, this country basket is filled with gleanings from the field, hedgerow and garden.

No rules here, just cram the basket to the brim with whatever you can find. Add a bunch or two from the market or florist if you've not enough at home.

Mixture of summer flowers such as
OLD FASHIONED GARDEN ROSES
DAHLIAS
BUDDLEIA
LARKSPUR
TRAHELIUM
MICHAELMAS DAISIES

From the field and hedgerow
WHEAT
ELDERBERRIES
ROWAN BERRIES
DOCK
YARROW
HAWTHORN

BASKET
FLORAL FOAM BRICKS
ALUMINIUM FOIL, PLASTIC BAG OR
CLING FILM

A basket can hold a huge quantity of flowers and, with the exception of large formal displays, flowers on this scale are rarely seen in the home. So treat yourself! If you have a garden, but little in it, try topping up what you have with a visit to the market or florist. You can fill the basket with foliage, berries and shrubs; even plants that are usually considered as weeds, if they take your fancy. Just aim to find as many different

A glorious selection from garden and hedgerow; this country-style basket is overflowing with blooms and berries, wheat and wild flowers. Use whatever you can find to load the basket full.

Roses in full bloom cluster at the front of the country basket. Use berries and wheat to hang gently over the front edge.

colours, textures, shapes and sizes of plants as possible. Leave the centre of the basket for the more beautiful blooms.

To protect the inside of the basket line it with aluminium foil and a plastic bag or cling film. Into this sit a brick or two (depending on the size of your basket) of well-soaked floral foam.

Begin the arrangement by slotting the longer stems, such as the larkspur, foliage and berries, around the edge.

Work one side, then the other, filling in a little at a time, aiming for good balance and harmony. Try to keep most of the flowers in groups. Don't be tempted to mix them up; the result will be a mess.

Build up the height of the basket with the longer-stemmed dahlias, trahelium and buddleia.

Now work the foreground, which is predominately a glorious mixture of garden roses in full bloom. Before you complete this section, tuck in clumps of wheat and berries which can drape gently over the front of the basket.

Always bear in mind to keep the display full, yet soft, with no harsh lines.

Finish off by adding the central flowers: roses and dahlia blooms.

HINT

The wonderful thing about this country-style basket is that because most of the flowers are grouped together, should some die, they can be removed and replaced with a fresh group.

Keep the foam wet and the basket should be long-lasting.

Line the basket with aluminium foil and a plastic bag to prevent any leakage from the soaked floral foam. Start the display by inserting long stems of foliage and flowers to one side of the basket.

Work the other side of the basket with clusters of the lovely mauve trahelium. Now begin to establish the height, selecting long-stemmed flowers such as dahlias. White dahlias are particularly lovely.

Work from side to side, filling the basket with clusters of flowers such as michaelmas daisies. Work towards the front with different-coloured roses. Tuck in wheat, elder and rowan berries to drape over the front edge.

Save the most beautiful roses till last, filling in at the front with a medley of colours and full-blown blooms. Finally add in clusters of berries or small groups of foliage to break up any solid lines.

Imitating art

Flower displays are frequently seen in works of art – from frescoes and mosaics, to paintings and sculptures. It can be well worth browsing through art books or galleries for some inspiration for your own flower arrangements.

Here, Van Gogh's evocative Sunflowers painting is the subject for a casual arrangement – the result is a wonderful imitation of the masterpiece.

SUNFLOWERS
STONEWARE JAR

In continental Europe, whole fields are filled with these fabulous flowers, all growing with their faces turning towards the sun. Yet as cut flowers, sunflowers prove to be difficult specimens. Their huge heads droop rapidly, especially in a very warm room. To counter this problem, look for the smaller sunflowers, about 60cm (2ft) high. Before you arrange them, lay them flat in a bath of cool water; the water is then absorbed along the length of the stem. This will give you a good, turgid stem with crisp leaves and a gently nodding flowerhead.

However, part of the beauty of sunflowers is their evocation of peasant countryside which is well expressed in their lax behaviour, their slightly drooping petals and rather distressed appearance.

Place the tallest stems in the jar first, then add shorter ones, working progressively down towards the shortest flowers at the front. Make sure you place the most prominent blooms in the centre, facing forwards. The fabulous central boss with its wide circular 'eye' should be shown to full advantage.

VARIATION
Create a miniature version of Van Gogh's Sunflowers with *Rudbeckia* – the smaller relatives of these lofty flowers. Look for the large, coarser varieties of *Rudbeckia* with their long fringes of petals and deep brown centres.

HINT
Sunflowers are easy to dry and look terrific in an autumnal arrangement. Simply hang the flowers upside down for about three weeks until the whole length of the stem has dried out. Test that the flowers are ready by feeling just beneath the flowerhead. The stem here should be completely dry.

Be inspired by the great masters. Van Gogh's most memorable Sunflowers painting is brought to life by the real thing.

Ice cream parlour

Pistachio and vanilla ice cream colours look fabulous set in aqua-tinted glass filled with water-green marbles. Paint-spray white carnations to match your decor.

Relatively inexpensive to buy and wonderfully long-lasting when cut, carnations appear in every florists shop, yet they are so often overlooked for a singular arrangement.

In this display, simple white carnations are mixed with those sprayed in a startling turquoise green to create a totally individual arrangement.

WHITE CARNATIONS
ASPARAGUS FERN
FLOWER PAINT
GREEN MARBLES
GLASS VASE

Flower paints are sold in large aerosol cans in well-stocked florists. They are available in a huge range of colours and can be great fun when used to enliven an everyday bunch.

Reminiscent of ice cream colours, the flowers look great set in recycled chunky greenish glass, with aqua coloured marbles used to give the display some added structure.

Spray the flowers first; they will not take long to dry. About one third of the flowers in this bunch were sprayed, the rest were left white.

Carefully fill the bottom of the vase with marbles, then add the water slowly; use a jug, it's easier.

Begin making a fairly traditional spray arrangement, creating an outline first and filling it in with the more open blooms. The marbles will help keep the stems in place. Space out the colours evenly, saving the best flowers for the foreground.

To break up the dense mass of flowers, tuck in little sprays of feathery fern.

HINT
Spray painting can be toxic, so read the instructions on the can. Always spray in a well-ventilated room or outside.

When you've finished spraying, turn the can upside down and continue to press the nozzle until only air comes out; this will ensure the paint doesn't dry out in the tube and render the can useless.

Build up a fairly traditional spray outline; shorter stems to the front, taller ones to the back. Tuck in a few stems of feathery fern to break up the solid line.

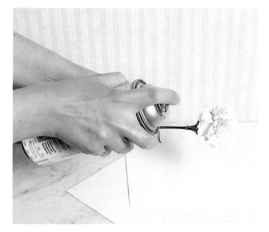

Aerosol paint can be quite messy, so hold the carnation over some paper to catch the paint mist. Spray the flowerhead following the manufacturer's instructions.

Colour craze

Add focus to any modern interior with an amazing contortion of paint-sprayed branches. Dazzlingly simple to execute, this design can work in any colour scheme; you just need plenty of space to admire it properly.

INTERESTING BRANCHES
CAR PAINT SPRAY IN WHITE AND THREE COLOURS
DRY FLORAL FOAM OR PEBBLES
MOSS
LARGE, SQUAT CONTAINER

This fantastic piece of modern interior design will last as long as you like; it will not fade, dry out or wilt. The worst that can happen is small bits snapping off.

Rescue prunings from trees or wind-fallen boughs, keeping your eyes open for really interesting, twisted shapes.

When you've accumulated sufficient branches – these ones were no more than 1m (3ft) in length – lay them out on to newspaper ready to paint. It's probably best to do this in the garden or a large garage, as the paint is quite toxic and, despite best efforts, tends to leave a slight film over nearby items.

Begin by spraying the branches white. Turn the branches as you spray. Don't be too fussy; an unevenness looks best.

When the branches are white – or almost so – and dry, start spraying them in the different colours you've chosen. Those here were painted in electric blue, orange and bright green. If you've plenty of time, strip the bark off first, as the final colour will be brighter.

Prepare your container – either packing it with some dry floral foam, or large, chunky pebbles, then push in the twigs until you're happy with the design. If you have used foam as your support, you will need to cover it with either some moss or some pretty pebbles.

Twisted branches in vivid green, electric blue and bright orange curl out of a beaten copper pot. The focus of a modern room, paint-sprayed branches become an art-form in their own right.

Antiquity

Few flowers can match the timeless quality and beauty of the rose. These lovely long-stemmed, ivory coloured roses have been mixed with the silvery seedheads of poppies to evoke a sense of grace, elegance and old-fashioned beauty.

LONG-STEMMED WHITE ROSES
NATURAL POPPY SEEDHEADS
OLD STONE VASE

This arrangement – which relies on the neck of the vase to give the display its support and shape – is simplicity itself. Use a fairly short, yet solid container, which will not be in danger of toppling.

With any long-stemmed plants it can be difficult for the water to travel all the way to the flowerhead unless you have conditioned them well. To prevent the rose heads from drooping, strip off the lower leaves, cut off the stem ends at an angle and either cut a slit up the stem or hammer the ends well. Let the flowers recover in a bucket of water in a cool place.

It's also worth adding a little cut flower conditioner to the water in the vase, as this will help preserve the display. Florists sell sachets of conditioner, or make your own (see page 110).

When the roses are ready, simply fill your vase with as many stems as you can; this display uses nearly 20 roseheads. Vary the heights slightly, keeping the taller stems to the centre of the vase. This gives a really full effect.

In among the roses, slot some poppy-heads. Because their stems are quite sturdy, dried poppies can be put into water among a fresh flower display.

VARIATIONS
Mixing dried and fresh flowers together can create attractive effects. Using this idea, why not combine different coloured roses with paint-sprayed poppyheads. Try lavender-coloured roses with blue poppyheads, deep yellow roses with gold sprayed poppyheads or apricot roses with peach-coloured poppyheads.

Ivory coloured long-stemmed roses and natural poppy seedheads fill a stoneware vase. The colours are cool and elegant.

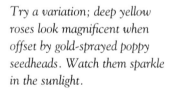

Try a variation; deep yellow roses look magnificent when offset by gold-sprayed poppy seedheads. Watch them sparkle in the sunlight.

PUSHING THE LIMITS

*Over the next few pages, you'll
find some of the very best floral
displays that can be achieved
simply, quickly and practically.
Whether for celebrations or
occasions or just to add a touch of
opulence to your home, here are
ideas and designs to inspire you.*

*Create a wedding swag of
Italianate ruffles from pure muslin,
adorned with tiny seed pearls and
pretty posies. Swathe your
mantelpiece this Christmas with
glossy green laurel, white lilies and
frosted hydrangeas – illuminated
with tiny, sparkling lights. Or
combine fresh and dried flowers
with seasonal fruits, heavy
brocades and rich tassels in a
sumptuous arrangement inspired
by the Renaissance. There's also a
wonderful idea for bringing to life
an empty summertime fireplace.*

Florentine swag

Flower swags have become increasingly popular for special occasions. This frothy creation, made from creamy-white muslin, is gathered in Italianate ruffles with pink ribbons and tiny pearls for the ultimate in wedding, christening or anniversary decorations.

Don't be daunted by either cost or skill, as neither are required in any measure. The swag is also lightweight, so suspending it from either a wall, shelf or table edge will cause no great damage.

Swag
MUSLIN
WIDE PALE PINK RIBBON
NARROW BRIGHT PINK RIBBON
STRING PEARLS
WHITE THREAD
WHITE TISSUE OR KITCHEN PAPER
FLORAL WIRE

This basic swag is made in about 15 minutes and can be decorated in a number of different ways.

The length of muslin recommended here makes a swag about 76cm (30in) across with proportional hanging drapes.

Begin by folding the muslin in half and tying a loose knot about 40cm (16in) either side of the halfway point.

Twist this middle section gently and gather up the muslin at regular intervals tying it with thread. This creates a series of little 'puffs'. Stuff some crumpled tissue or kitchen paper into the puffs.

This forms the basic swag shape. At this stage, it's best to add the ribbon, then suspend the swag and work on it in situ.

Using both the wider pale pink ribbon and the narrow bright pink ribbon, twirl them around the swag, allowing the ends to trail down each side. The string pearls are wound round in the same way. As this display is asymmetrical, allow the pearls to cascade down the left-hand side of the

A delicate, gauzy, muslin swag is decorated with pretty posies of pink rosebuds and gypsophila. It makes the perfect highlight for the celebration table.

swag and finish at the knot on the right.

At this point, you'll find it easier to hang the swag in position. To do this, you'll need to push a small piece of wire through the swag at the back of each muslin knot and twist the ends together to make a loop.

Gently knock two panel pins or picture nails into the wall where the knots of the swag will be, allowing for a gentle drape in the centre. The wire loops can then be hooked on.

Decorating the swag
PINK ROSES
PINK AND WHITE ROSEBUDS
GYPSOPHILA
PALE PINK TULIPS

Once you've established the middle section of the swag, create a series of puffs by tying the muslin tightly at regular intervals with white sewing thread.

Gather a selection of flowers in one hand, rearranging them until you are happy with the effect. Secure the posy by winding the stems with floral tape.

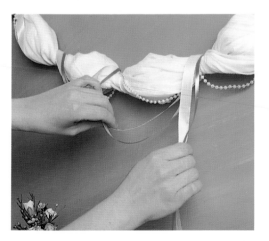

Take wide and narrow ribbon together and twist them around the centre of the swag. Allow sufficient ribbon on both sides so that it can trail down.

The larger clusters are fixed to the swag with a little floral wire. Wind it tightly around the stems then again around the muslin. Twist the ends together to finish.

PALE PINK CARNATIONS
PINK WAX FLOWERS
FLORAL TAPE
FLORAL WIRE
WIDE PINK SATIN RIBBON
WIDE BURGUNDY RIBBON

To achieve a good balance, create a large group of flowers on the left-hand knot of the muslin. Use the larger roses and gather up small rosebuds and gypsophila around them. Tape the group together. Once the cluster is in place you can add other flowers and tiny bows made from burgundy ribbon.

A smaller group sits on the opposite knot. Use the same flowers, just fewer of them, to give a sense of continuity.

The other smaller clusters are made in the same way. Finish off with loops of wider satin ribbon, gathered together with a twist of wire and pushed in among the posies to cover any gaps.

HINT
Mist the flowers with water to keep them looking fresh.

The dominant cluster used large pink roses as its focal point offset by tiny pink and white rosebuds and cloudy sprays of gypsophila.

Fill out the flower clusters and cover any visible tape or stems by pushing in individual flowers. They will be held in place by the already-positioned posies.

The smaller flower clusters can simply be slipped into the folds of the muslin, although you might want to add a little wire twisted around for extra security.

Making an entrance

First impressions are lasting impressions – so make a truly breathtaking one.

Lofty stems of electric blue and purple delphiniums stand above plump peonies in a classical Chinese-style jar.

This early summer mixture of flowers comes straight from the garden, with perhaps one or two additions from the florist, so it needn't cost a fortune.

DELPHINIUMS
EREMURUS
LILIES
PEONIES
STOCKS
LIZZIEANTHUS
WIRE MESH
TALL JAR

Designed to stand on the floor, this display would be perfect for an entrance hall or lobby, or the lee of a bay window.

Scrunch up some plastic coated wire mesh and squeeze it into the jar. This will enable you to position the flowers as you wish, as flowers have an uncanny knack of moving by themselves!

Start with the tall stems: the delphiniums and the *Eremurus*.

Delphiniums are available in a wide variety of blue and purple hues, from the palest mauve to the brightest azure. On the lighter colours, the deep indigo eye at the centre of the flower is most impressive.

With the taller flowers in place add long stems of sweet-smelling stock. Use deep magenta stock as a colour harmonizer; it helps bring together the purple and pink colours.

The peonies form the focal point. Recess some to give added depth.

Fill in the outline with tall stems of mixed stocks and purple lizzieanthus. One or two lilies add interest and a contrast in texture.

Lofty stems of delphiniums and Eremurus create a lordly display for the lobby or entrance hall. Or use this floor-standing arrangement to highlight a bay window.

The delphiniums and Eremurus stand proud. Arrange them to fan out from the tall jar, placing the gently curving stems of the Eremurus to the outer edges.

Use the peonies to create a focal point in the centre of the display. Save three or four blooms to recess among the other flowers. These will add depth and substance.

Summertime fireplace

A mixture of misty blues and purples fill a fireplace during the summer. A nice touch is to hang drying flowers from the mantelpiece. Here, globe artichokes blend with the flowers of the display.

Summer's fireplace – with its yawning black hole – is best disguised. Use bounteous quantities of dried flowers such as sea lavender, hydrangeas, statice and pearl everlasting, and transform an eyesore into a spectacular display which will last you all summer through.

SEA LAVENDER
PALE AND BRIGHT MAUVE STATICE
BLUE MOP-HEAD HYDRANGEAS
PEARL EVERLASTING
GLOBE ARTICHOKES
SEA HOLLY
FLORAL FOAM BRICK

Any large arrangement will use a vast quantity of flowers. To keep the cost down, use inexpensive flowers – sea lavender and statice – as your main ingredients.

There are various types of sea lavender available – all known botanically as *Limonium*. Look for – *L. caspia* – the type which is misty blue and bears feathery sprays. It is also known as large-flowered sea lavender. This gives a softer outline than the coarser, more wiry, type which bears tiny clusters of creamy white flowers (*L. tataricum*). This display uses both types of sea lavender.

Statice is of the same botanical family, but is known as *Limonium sinuatum*. It has a bright colour range including yellow, purple, white, pink and blue.

Mop-head hydrangeas make wonderful dried specimens, although the red ones dry with a stronger colour than the blue. So cheat a little. Take last year's flowerheads and spray them with a sky blue flower or car paint.

Gather the flowers together in front of the fireplace. As they shed so much when you're cutting them to length, put them on to sheets of newspaper.

Insert a brick or two of dry floral foam into the grate and begin slotting in the sea lavender. Build up a full outline, letting it drape over the front of the grate and out at the sides. Continue to fill out the shape you've established, using clumps of statice and pearly everlasting.

With the background more or less in place, insert four or five hydrangea heads towards the centre. Leave some gaps to add in more clusters of statice and pearly everlasting. Use the deep purple statice to good effect here. Paradoxically, it provides brightness and depth.

Slot in the artichoke heads at an angle.

As a final note, lighten this display with little sprays of blue sea holly.

The dried artichoke stems are thick and tough, and need quite a bit of persuasion to push into place. Globe artichokes make exotic dried plants, adding texture and weight.

The statice makes a wonderful infill flower. Keep the stems short and bunch the linear flowerheads close together; in this way the display is quickly filled with clumps of colour.

Romance

Celebrate a wedding or engagement with a fairytale display of delicate pink rosebuds and blushing jasmine.

The design is cleverly formed around a wire sconce which has also been used as a curtain tie back.

A perfect backdrop to the bridal table at the wedding breakfast, this romantic arrangement can be constructed swiftly and will last well beyond the day's celebrations.

For the drapes
PINK PRINTED VOILE
DOUBLE-SIDED TAPE
WIRE WALL SCONCE

While this display looks perfectly lovely by itself, the frame of gauzy curtains is undoubtedly an attractive feature. For such a special occasion, it's worth creating some mock curtains to act as a backdrop.

Measure the height of your wall, double it and add on an extra metre (yard). This will give you plenty of fabric, even if it is only 90cm (36in) wide.

Cut the extra metre or yard from the end of the fabric and cut the remaining piece into two equal lengths. Stick lines of double-sided tape to the wall and hang the fabric from this.

Gather the fabric slightly at the top so that it hangs in gentle folds.

Hang the sconce on the wall in between the fabric. Use a panel pin or picture hook if there isn't a convenient one already in the wall; this can be gently eased out afterwards, leaving virtually no lasting mark.

Gather the drapes into the sconce and let them flow through.

As the top edge of the drapes will probably look as if it has just been stuck on the wall – which of course it has – disguise it with the remaining piece of fabric. Fold in the raw edges and loop the fabric gently above the top of the drapes. Stick it in place with small pieces of double-sided tape.

For the flower sprays
PALE PINK ROSES AND ROSEBUDS
JASMINE
IVY
SPRENGERI OR ASPARAGUS FERN
FLORAL FOAM

With the sconce and drapes in position, begin the display in earnest. Cut cubes of floral foam and soak them well. Squash them on to the candleholders. Where possible, squeeze a little more foam on to other parts of the sconce. This one has a central basket into which a small brick of foam was placed.

Use trailing stems of ivy to curl down the sconce, twisting it in and out of the wire. Bear in mind that the arrangement is an asymmetrical one and also that you do not want to cover the wire completely.

Try to find the pink-tipped jasmine; sometimes known as Chinese jasmine, as this is such a pretty complement to the pale pink roses. Follow the lines of the ivy, but keep some of the stems shorter, to form an outline around each of the foam pieces.

Fill in with rosebuds and open blooms, saving the best ones for the centre of the display.

Stand back occasionally to assess your work; it's easy to adjust the balance as you go along. Fill any gaps with small stems of jasmine or little rosebuds.

For a final soft touch, tuck in a few stems of feathery fern.

VARIATION
Use yellow-printed voile drapes, yellow tea roses and yellow trailing jasmine or honeysuckle.

Gauzy sheer fabric drapes set the scene for a romantic collection of pale pink roses and trailing jasmine.

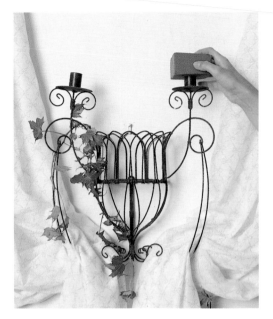

With the drapes and sconce in position, push blocks of floral foam on to the sconce. Use adhesive tape if there are no convenient points to hold the foam. Twist trailing stems of ivy down through the wire.

Pale pink-tipped jasmine, also known as Chinese jasmine, is a wonderful complement to the roses. Use ivy to trail down and give the arrangement some contrast of texture.

Create clusters of roses and jasmine to cover the foam blocks. Use plenty of rose and jasmine foliage; not only does it add depth, but the jasmine can be trained down and around the wire.

Save the open rose blooms for the focal points of the display. Condition the stems well before arranging them; this will prevent the flowerheads from drooping. Mist them lightly once the display is complete.

Winter sideboard

Fake is great! New-style fake flowers and fruits are in vogue in a big way. Plump pomegranates and quinces are sprayed boldly in silver or gold, berries can be bought in emerald green or snow white, while damsons and cherries look lifelike with their heavy mock patina. Fabric flowers are either realistic or unashamedly false with glitzy petals and crystal stamens.

Fake lasts forever, so it's worth splashing out on a collection of pieces which can be used again and again. Mix them with shiny paper ribbon or glittery sequin waste for a truly spectacular piece.

FAKE FOLIAGE
SELECTION OF SMALL FAKE FRUITS
LARGE FAKE FRUITS SPRAYED SILVER
TINY SILVER BAUBLES
INDIGO-COLOURED SILK FLOWERS
BLACK SEQUIN WASTE
BLACK NET
GREEN SHINY PAPER RIBBON

FLORAL WIRE
DRY FLORAL FOAM
FLORAL ADHESIVE TAPE
RECTANGULAR TRAY

This display uses purple and green as its two main colours; silver is used for highlights.

You should be able to buy fake fruit all year round from a specialist floral supplier. But at Christmas time even department stores and florists will stock a wide range of pretend fruits and berries.

Look out for both highly artificial pieces – those sprayed silver or gold – as well as the more authentic types which may be the same size and colour as the real fruit, even down to the bloom on the skin. Collect as many as you can of varying sizes.

For a good range of fake foliage, you'll need to find a floral supplier. Look out for plastic covered wire stems supporting fabric leaves which look almost real. Don't worry if these come in a big bunch; individual stems can be snipped off with wirecutters.

Paper ribbon and sequin waste can be bought from stationers as well as floral suppliers. Shiny paper ribbon should be available all year round.

With everything assembled, start the display by taping two dry foam bricks to the small, rectangular tray. Use the floral

Add a few flowers to one side of the display. Mix glittery blooms with plain ones of the same shade for a pretty effect. These flowers often come on long stems bearing several blooms. Snip them into smaller sprays.

Use the larger fruits for the focal point of the display, slotting them in towards the front. Vary the angles at which you position them to add interest. Intersperse them with little clusters of smaller fruits or berries.

adhesive tape; any other kind will not stick. Place one foam brick on its side, stand the other up on its end, and trim off the top. You should end up with an outline that looks like an 'L' lying down.

Take an oblong piece of black net and scrunch it up into a loose sausage shape. Fold the sausage into two loops and bind the base of the loops together tightly with wire. Twist the ends together to form a tail. This can be pushed into the foam later. Tease the net apart for a filmy effect.

Build up an outline with several of these net loops and foliage. Snip the foliage into individual stems bearing several leaves to give you more scope.

Now start inserting the smaller fruits among the foliage and net. In among the fruits, insert individual stems of tiny 'grapes', grouping them in twos or threes.

Use the fake flowers sparingly. Position a few out to one side, backing them up with trailing foliage and net.

Add the larger pieces of fruit to the front as the focal point. Tuck small pieces of fruit or a leaf in between them.

Finally, use the shiny ribbon, silver baubles and sequin waste for highlights. The ribbon and sequin waste are gathered into loops like the net.

Gently tease apart the paper ribbon and gather it into two or three loops. Bind the loops at the base with wire, then ease the loops open to create a rich double bow.

Fabulous fake fruits and flowers jostle together amidst filmy black net and shiny sequin waste. Add highlights with silver baubles and silver-sprayed fake pomegranates.

Harvest urn

As summer fades into autumn, flowers become more scarce and expensive. This is the season when chrysanthemums come into their own. Widely available at this time of year, they always evoke the mellowness of autumn – their warm hues reflecting the changing colours of the leaves.

The florists' pompon chrysanthemums or 'blooms' are perhaps the ultimate variety. Mix them with smaller flowers and a pyramid of bronze-skinned applies in a stone or metal urn for a harvest or Thanksgiving celebration.

CREAM 'BLOOM' CHRYSANTHEMUMS
ORANGE AND DEEP RED CHRYSANTHEMUMS
APPLES
LAUREL
WOODEN SKEWERS
FLORAL FOAM
URN

Look out for ornamental urns in garden stores or even architectural salvage dealers or junk shops. Outdoor urns can look just as effective inside, and they make the perfect container for a wide range of fabulous flower displays.

As an urn is usually heavy, made from metal or stone, put it into position first. Soak some bricks of floral foam; it will depend on the size of the urn, but half a brick wedged at the bottom will then support another brick, standing on its end. Let the second brick protrude above the rim of the urn by at least half to enable you to construct a pyramid shape.

Form a basic outline with the cream bloom chrysanthemums. If this display is front-facing only, you will not need to worry about the back; if it's to be seen from all sides, you will have to allow for more flowers and fruit.

Push a wooden skewer into the apple (bearing in mind which part of the fruit you want to be visible) and push the other end of the skewer into the foam. Build the apples into a pyramid shape, recessing them behind the cream blooms.

Use the red and orange chrysanthemums to fill out the basic shape. As these are the most inexpensive flowers, you can be quite generous in the amount you use.

Finish off with small sprays of laurel or other shiny evergreen leaves. This breaks up the rather heavy mass and lifts the display. Let a couple of stems drape over the rim of the urn.

Golden-skinned apples and autumn chrysanthemums are piled high in a garden urn. The large cream chrysanthemum blooms really steal the show.

You can buy wooden skewers in larger supermarkets. Choose the best side of the apple to be seen and push the pointed end of the skewer into the other side of the fruit.

Build up the arrangement, filling in with stems of red and orange chrysanthemums. Tuck the darker blooms well in to the display to create depth and to cover any visible foam.

Caravaggio

Deep wine reds and sumptuous claret colours combine in this rich, classical masterpiece. Tiny grapes hang from the cherub's basin and flowers mingle with ripe pomegranates and figs. Little rosebuds and glossy burgundy and gold ribbon cascade in a display worthy of the most special of occasions.

Although a little more timely to assemble than some of the other arrangements, this display is methodically constructed and is a wonderful outlet for your creative talents.

PURPLE CHRYSANTHEMUMS
BURGUNDY-COLOURED CARNATIONS
WHITE CARNATIONS TINGED WITH
BURGUNDY
GOLD-SPRAYED TEASELS
DRIED RED HYDRANGEA HEADS
SHINY EVERGREEN FOLIAGE
PROTEA COMPACTA BUDS
CREAM SPIDER CHRYSANTHEMUMS
RED ROSES
FIGS
POMEGRANATES
VINE LEAVES WITH GRAPES

WIDE GOLD AND BURGUNDY RIBBON
STUB WIRE
COCKTAIL STICKS
FLORAL FOAM TABLETS
STICKY FIXERS
CAKE PILLARS
CAKE BOARDS
CHERUB VASE

You could style this arrangement on stacking cake stands, to create a layer of tiers from which the flowers cascade. However, it's probably easier to use commercial cake boards – the thin variety in silver or preferably gold – and little pillars or columns to support them.

The cake boards used here measure 20cm (8in) and 30cm (12in) in diameter.

Straight from the realms of myth and fantasy; this rich and opulent display would be Bacchus' delight. Tiny bunches of grapes and vine leaves cascade amidst golden ribbon and tiny red rosebuds, while burgundy carnations and exotic protea buds frame golden teasels and bursting pomegranate fruits.

Begin by standing four pillars in position ready for the arrangement. Make sure they're equidistant and put the larger cake board on top, readjusting the pillars as necessary. When you're happy with their position, attach a sticky fixer to the top of each pillar then push the cake board firmly on top.

In the centre of the board, place a well soaked tablet of floral foam and position three more cake pillars around it to support the next layer. However, don't put the second cake board on top yet.

Start with the hydrangeas and carnations, packing them into the sides of the foam, allowing some to drape well over the edge of the cake board. Push in the teasels and to one side add the long protea buds.

The exotic protea are a dried-flower arranger's delight. Most well-stocked suppliers should have them. In fact, with the growing demand for unusual plant material, many suppliers now hold a wide range of different seedpods and dried plants from all over the world.

Insert longer stems of purple chrysanthemums to the sides; you should aim to create width as well as covering the front where the lower pillars are supporting the board.

Fruits added to any display create an air of bounty and opulence. In this arrangement, pomegranates and figs have been slotted in among the flowers using cocktail sticks to secure them into the foam (see page 111).

On this lower level add a pomegranate sliced in half to reveal its glistening ruby red seeds. Mist well with water to keep it looking moist and fresh.

Fill in this lower level with stems of foliage – laurustinus (*Viburnum tinus*) looks pretty, especially if it's in flower – and generous ribbon bows. To add the ribbon, you'll need to wire it first (full

The rich and heavy colours are lifted by the pale spider chrysanthemums. The light pomegranate skin also adds a contrast of colour.

Position four cake pillars in place and secure the larger cake board to each one with a sticky fixer. On top of the board, place a well-soaked tablet of floral foam.

instructions appear on page 111).

Apply some sticky fixers to the top three cake pillars and press down the smaller cake board. It should fit comfortably on to the other layer with out any visible gaps.

Slice a foam tablet in half to create a slim circle, soak it well and place it in the centre of the smaller cake board. Sit the cherub vase on top of the foam. (You might need a bigger piece of foam, depending on what size vase you can find. These plastic cherub vases are available from good floral wholesalers.)

Now begin the second layer, using more hydrangeas, foliage and carnations, but also adding two sprays of red roses and some figs. To secure the figs, push them gently on to a cocktail stick and insert the other end into the foam. They look delicious if you cut one in half to expose the tiny seeds.

Complete this final layer with a small

ribbon bow and two or three cream spider chrysanthemums; these add bright highlights to an otherwise solid mess of dark colours.

To finish, fill the cherub's vase with tiny bunches of home-grown grapes and autumn vine leaves (small red seedless grapes can substitute), a half pomegranate and a collection of chrysanthemums and foliage.

HINT
Keep the display well misted to preserve its freshness.

VARIATION
If you are unable to find a little cherub vase – don't be too despairing. Use an old-fashioned, heavy wine glass instead. As the support will be seen through the glass, use a pinholder to keep the flowers in place; it's much less obtrusive than dark green foam.

Work first on the lower layer of flowers, fruit, foliage and ribbon. Create width and depth, using longer stems of carnations, chrysanthemums and the exotic protea buds.

Build up the layer with more of the same flowers, but add in the teasels, ribbon bows. A pomegranate to one side adds to the air of opulence. Slice it open to reveal its seeds.

LAST
MINUTE
IDEAS

*If you're in a hurry, need a quick
gift idea, or want to put a little
flourish to a last minute dinner
party – this is the chapter
to read.*

*There are pretty little flower
baskets to put together in minutes
using fresh or dried flowers. Make
a memento napkin tie with herbs
from the garden or supermarket.
Or give a miniature rose – bought
hurriedly from a petrol station – a
swift makeover with little ribbons
and swathes of giftwrap and
colourful tissue.*

*You'll also find even more
suggestions and variations on every
project page to give you a host of
quick and easy ideas.*

Elizabethan herb napkin

Twisted gold and crimson cord is knotted simply round a bunch of mixed, fresh herbs for an eleventh-hour table decoration.

Use herbs from the garden or window-box, making use of any flowering varieties. If you haven't any home grown herbs, try the supermarket. Most stock a selection of fresh herbs in the chiller cabinet. As you'll not find any flowering herbs, add stems of lavender for colour.

Mixed fresh herbs
CHIVES
ROSEMARY
THYME
SAGE
MINT
OREGANO/MARJORAM
LEMON BALM

FLORAL TWIST
DECORATIVE CORD

A small bunch of mixed, fresh herbs makes a wonderfully aromatic napkin tie. It's also a practical memento for your guests to take home with them.

Gather a selection of mixed herbs. Use whatever you have to hand, although look for interesting-shaped leaves and any flowering varieties which will make the bunch that bit more attractive. Don't forget plants like lavender, which can also be included.

Arrange the bunch into an interesting display. Hold it tightly in one hand, then twist a wire florists' tie around the bunch to secure it.

Loosely fold the napkin into a fan shape and place the herb bunch on top. Tie the cord around the napkin and herbs, finishing with a decorative reef knot. Trim the ends of the cord and knot them once to prevent them from fraying.

VARIATION
This principle can be adapted in a number of ways. Use small bunches of dried flowers; lavender and tiny red roses are very attractive together. Tie them into the napkin with a matching mauve or red ribbon. Alternatively, use silk or parchment flowers tied to the napkin with plaited embroidery threads or braid.

HINT
Many herbs are easy to grow in windowsill pots or troughs. In fact, many supermarkets sell herbs in pots which can be transplanted to a larger container. Invest in a herb growers' guide and you may be surprised how quickly you become addicted to this miniature form of gardening. Apart from cooking and last-minute gift or decoration ideas, home-grown herbs will emit a lovely scent.

Gather the herbs together; arranging them to form an attractive bunch. Take a florists' green wire twist and secure the bunch tightly. The wire twist will be disguised by the decorative cord.

A small selection of garden herbs are gathered into a bunch and placed on to a fresh, white napkin. Tie the two together with a length of knotted cord or braid.

Clevbus Vernus.

Early Flowering Orobus, or Bitter Vetch.

; the
es, (of which
, the
lowers, Daffodil
flower'; some othe
e:, will blossom befo
ong these are the co
, lungwort, with its gree
bells, some pink, so
rs dark blue.; the Canad
her a scarce plant.) Fritillar
kinds, Orobus vernus, (a small yell
my taste, the prettiest early herba

Mini landscape

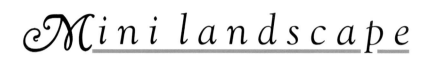

Cool and fresh, this miniature landscape suggests the tranquillity of a gently lapping water's edge.

It's easily constructed from ordinary glass tumblers and large grey pebbles. Poolside flowers like irises and the graceful stems of pampas or bear grass set the scene.

For an elegant final touch, knot a piece of grass around each napkin.

IRISES
PAMPAS OR BEAR GRASS
GREY PEBBLES
SELECTION OF GLASS TUMBLERS
CLEAR GLASS MARBLES
FINE WIRE

Many people collect pretty pebbles or stones from seaside holidays. These cool grey stones, veined in white and ochre, re-create a lapping lakeside.

Set five or six different-sized tumblers in place directly on to the table (a tablecloth would spoil this effect; a natural surface such as scrubbed pine or beech looks so much better).

Pile the pebbles around the glasses, until you're satisfied with the result. Try to hide most of the tumblers with the stones.

Carefully load each tumbler with clear glass marbles and, using a jug, top up each one with water.

Into each tumbler, insert one or maybe two irises. Cut the stems down as necessary and try to position the flower so that it stands upright.

Conjuring up images of the Orient, the simple lines of this arrangement are the secrets of its success. Use glass tumblers of varying heights, disguised with waterside pebbles. The tiny sprays of grass and the occasional iris flower completes the display. No one would realise that it's put together in minutes!

Add the grass. It's less painstaking if you twist a little wire around three or four stems of grass first. These thin bunches can then be pushed in among the marbles.

For the napkins
PAMPAS OR BEAR GRASS
ONE OR TWO IRIS FLOWERS
COARSE LINEN OR COTTON NAPKINS

Fold the napkins into four and then into three to give you a simple rectangular shape.

Take a long piece of grass and wrap it once around the centre of the napkin. Although the grass is quite strong, you will need to take care that it does not snap. Tie the grass into a knot at the front of the napkin, then snip off the ends.

You can also slip an iris flower into the grass tie on the occasional napkin. However, in keeping with the image of the arrangement leave most of the napkins plain.

Make simple napkin ties from pieces of bear or pampas grass. Tuck an iris flower in the occasional napkin to add variety.

Assemble several glass tumblers of differing heights and pile up the pebbles around them. Fill each tumbler with clear marbles and top up with water.

Fruited boughs

The fruits of late summer and early autumn make a stylish display with virtually no arranging at all.

Set the twisting branches of a crab or wild apple into an Oriental-style umbrella stand; it's an instant art form.

Stand it in the hallway or enliven a boring corner of the room.

BRANCHES BEARING FRUIT
HACKSAW
HAMMER
WIRE MESH
REINDEER MOSS
UMBRELLA STAND

Crab apple trees are frequently ignored on almost every front; yet the fruit makes wonderful jelly, and the trees are small but splendidly ornamental in any garden. Their branches also look fabulous set in a tall container against a slatted screen or Venetian blind.

Carefully saw off two or three smaller, fruit-bearing branches. The branches shouldn't be too thick, otherwise you can't hammer the ends. You'll need to do this if you want the leaves to last a little; they wither quickly otherwise. (See page 109 for conditioning tips).

Fill the umbrella stand with water and crumpled mesh. Put it into position – it's difficult to move once the branches are in place. Push the branches in among the mesh. They can topple easily, so you'll need to push them in hard and make sure they are steady before you add the next.

Take handfuls of reindeer moss or lichen and cover any bits of visible wire mesh. (Reindeer moss is plentiful in coniferous forests. It grows in clumps on the branches.)

VARIATION

Try japonica or other type of quince. In spring use boughs of sweet-smelling blossom.

HINT

If the fruit falls off during transit – cheat! Use a hot glue gun (useful for dried flower arranging) and stick the fruit back on to the twigs. Alternatively, use some green floral wire; twist it around the stem of the fruit and on to the branch.

Heavy branches of wild apple create an Oriental look, especially if set in a tall Chinese pot and backed with a simple screen.

Tie and dry

Give kitchen shelves or a pine dresser a country look with small hanging bunches of dried or drying flowers.

Tie each bunch with something different; use string, twine, fabric, ribbon, wool, braid, lace; the list goes on!

This makes good use of small bunches of dried flowers and it gives you somewhere to hang any pieces you want to dry yourself.

SELECTION OF FLOWERS, EITHER DRIED
OR TO DRY
SELECTION OF TIES
RUBBER BANDS
DRAWING OR PANEL PINS

Many flowers can be successfully dried by hanging them upside down out of direct sunlight. If you want to dry your own flowers, check first that they can be preserved in this way (see Air drying, page 112). Good examples include roses, strawflowers, statice, sunray, gypsophila, or any seedheads.

Gather just a few specimens together and secure them into a bunch with a rubber band. As the stems shrink when they dry out, a rubber band keeps the bunch together. You can then add a more decorative tie on top.

You can also use ready-dried bunches of flowers. Leftovers from larger arrangements can be used up this way. You'll not need to tie them with a rubber band first.

You will probably have an amazingly wide array of suitable ties in the home; anything goes! Look in the sewing box for ribbon, braid, wool, lace or cord. In the garden shed you might have twine, string or raffia. Twine, cord or wool can be plaited to give a thicker tie.

There are also oddments of fabric: these don't need sewing; simply fold them into narrow lengths ready for tying.

Use giftwrapping ribbon, or pieces of net or hessian.

And why not buy some pieces? Try paper ribbon. This comes in tight coils which must be teased apart before treating it like ordinary wide ribbon. It creates a spectacular effect, even though it is quite expensive.

Another alternative is one of the lovely wired ribbons. These have narrow casings down each side filled with fine wire. When you've tied your bow, you can tug it into any shape; the wire will hold it in place.

Hang the bunches from the shelves with fine drawing or panel pins, or use existing cup hooks. Lightweight bunches can even be attached using sticky fixers of double-sided tape.

VARIATION
Decorating with little bunches needn't be reserved for the kitchen shelves. Hang flowers from an old-fashioned clothes airer or wooden beams on the ceiling. Bunches containing santolina, lavender, southernwood or tansy are good moth and insect deterrents; hang them by a wardrobe or linen cupboard.

HINT
Store a selection of fabrics, ribbons and other bits and pieces in clean plastic bags. Not only can they come in handy for this project, but they are also useful to create a quick, hand-tied bouquet of dried or fresh flowers. Gathered together and bound with a flamboyant paper bow, or a piece of plaited braid, for example, they can look most attractive.

Adorn kitchen shelves with a selection of dried or drying flowers all tied in a motley collection of different things. Use braid, twine, raffia, ribbon, wool, paper ribbon, golden cord and scraps of printed fabric.

Miniature potted rose

These make such lovely gifts. Whether they are put out into a patio pot, or kept indoors, they outlast any fresh bouquet.

On sale at most florists, supermarkets and even petrol stations, miniature roses are relatively inexpensive to buy, yet will delight most friends or relations.

Make your rose just a little bit special by adorning it with tiny bows and wrapping it in cloudy tissue and floral giftwrap. So simple, it can even be done *en route*!

MINIATURE ROSE PLANT
NARROW RIBBON
TISSUE PAPER
GIFTWRAP

A potted miniature rose is given a little extra decorative treatment. Using either giftwrap ribbon or satin ribbon, tie little bows to the stems of the rose plant. Send the giftwrap ribbon into tiny curls by running a scissor blade along it. These dainty plants are readily available from florists, supermarkets and petrol stations and make an excellent solution for a last-minute gift idea.

Most of these miniature rose plants come in a cellophane sleeve. Remove this and trim off any yellowing or dead leaves or buds. If you've time, mist it with a little water.

Cut several lengths of narrow ribbon; use a coordinating colour if you can, and tie them to the stems of the plant in little bows.

You can use ordinary dressmaking, satin ribbon or giftwrap ribbon. Here, both have been used. The advantage of giftwrap ribbon is that it can be pulled into attractive little coils. To do this, tie the ribbon around the stem, then run a scissor blade swiftly along the 'tails' of the ribbon, from the knot to the end. It will spring into curls.

There is an excellent selection of gift wrapping papers on the market, so it's worth seeking out one of the shiny floral ones. If you can find one with roses on – usually no problem – all the better. One sheet is all you will need.

Lay the wrapping paper face up and place a couple of sheets of coloured tissue paper on top at an angle. Try to use a coordinating or contrasting colour, although green always works well with any plant.

Sit the rose in the centre of the wrapping and simply gather the paper up around it. Peel the paper back at the top to reveal the rose.

VARIATION
Use the giftwrap as your inspiration – there are heaps of good ideas. For example, a daffodil paper could be lined with yellow or green tissue and filled with potted narcissi. Tie big yellow bows around the stems.

Pretty mauve/blue hydrangea giftwrapping paper could be lined with lilac tissue to present a potted blue hydrangea plant.

Instant pot pourri

This is a lovely way to use up wilting roses, whether summertime ones or the forced hybrid tea roses sold during the winter months.

The flowerheads and petals will slowly dry out, retaining their exquisite shapes and deepening in colour. Add a little pot pourri oil to enhance the petals' own scent and either keep it for yourself, or present it in an attractive shallow container as a gift.

ROSEHEADS AND LOOSE PETALS
SHALLOW DISH
ROSE ESSENTIAL OIL

So simple and so very attractive. When still fresh, the roseheads have a tissue-like quality which is quite beautiful. As they dry out, the petals become crisper and deeper in colour, but they lose none of their beauty.

Look for a shallow glass or china dish, which will show off the flowers to their best advantage.

Take wilting roses and snip off their heads. Keep the loveliest roses intact. Pull the petals from the others.

Fill the dish with the petals and stir in two or three drops of rose oil. This is very strong; you'll only need a little for any pot pourri mix.

Top up the dish with roseheads and tiny rosebuds.

As the flowers dry out, add a little more oil to reinforce the scent.

For a gift
Cover the filled dish with cling film and tie with a pretty matching ribbon.

As a lovely alternative, make a green herb pot pourri using garden or potted herbs or even those from the supermarket. The herbs dry out naturally. Crush a few leaves to release their wonderful aroma.

Soft rose petals and wilting rose heads create an instant pot pourri. They dry in situ, deepening in colour and preserving their attractive shape. Enhance their natural smell with a few drops of essential rose oil.

Save the most beautiful specimens and keep them whole. Strip the petals from the more bedraggled roseheads and use these to fill up the dish.

Flower baskets

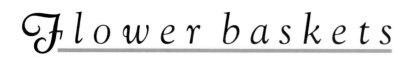

Little baskets are generally inexpensive yet they can be so useful. Here, filled to the brim with flowers, they make the perfect present.

Use whatever flowers you have to hand, or those which are easy to buy. The ones selected here should give you some inspiration. Each basket is simple and quick to assemble and won't cost a fortune.

Fresh flower basket
ROSES
LAVENDER
NARCISSI
EVERGREEN FOLIAGE
FLORAL FOAM
BASKET

Roses and lavender make good companions, and as they're common garden flowers you should have no problem gathering enough for a small basket. The narcissi add a delicate touch with their papery white petals; this variety are sometimes known as paper lights.

Soak the foam well and slot it into the basket. Make a full outline from the foliage and the pretty little narcissi; the display should be no higher than the basket's handle, but should extend out slightly each side. Slot in some stems of lavender, leaving the central area for the roses. Fill in any gaps with foliage sprays.

Potted plant
MINIATURE CYCLAMEN
BASKET
PAPER RIBBON

You could use any potted, flowering plant. Chrysanthemums, particularly the small marguerites, African violets, miniature roses or begonias will all look even more attractive if popped into a basket.

Although it may sound painfully obvious, do make sure that before you buy the plant your chosen basket will accommodate it.

For a flourishing touch, decorate the basket with white paper ribbon or, alternatively, fill it first with shredded tissue in a complementary colour to the blooms. Let the tissue spill out over the rim before placing the plant inside.

Dried flower basket
DRIED BROOM BLOOM IN TWO COLOURS
DRIED YELLOW ROSES
GREEN REINDEER MOSS
FLORAL FOAM
HESSIAN RIBBON
BASKET

Broom bloom comes in a fabulous array of dyed colours; emerald green and cream make a lovely foil for dried yellow roses. Pack the basket with dry floral foam and fill it with the broom bloom, keeping the two colours in clusters. Dot the yellow roses throughout the broom bloom. Tuck the reindeer moss round the rim of the basket to camouflage any visible stems and finish with a natural-style hessian bow on the basket's handle.

HINT
Little wicker baskets are inexpensive, yet come in a wide range of styles and designs. If you see one you like, buy it to save for later; for last minute ideas, like these, it can come in extremely useful. Apart from florists, baskets can be bought in beauty stores, variety shops and home interiors or department stores.

Three delightful little flower baskets: for absolutely no fuss, pop a small potted plant into a basket and decorate it with paper ribbon; the dried and fresh flower baskets take a little longer but use only elementary flower arranging skills.

CHOOSING & CARING

Like all living things, flowers need tender loving care. Even cut ones can last longer if given the correct treatment.
This final chapter is a ready reference to flower arranging. What tools and equipment are really necessary? What are the time-saving tips and techniques? And how can you dry and preserve your own flowers. There's also an easy-to-access chart of the most popular flowers, how to condition them and ways to use them to their best advantage.

Equipment

If you've struggled to keep a display in place, or have desperately tried to cut tough stems with manicure scissors, you'll know that using the right tools for the job makes life so much easier.

There are plenty of tools and pieces of equipment on the market for the would-be florist. But as flower arranging has become less tortured and more free, so some of the tools of the trade are only for specialist displays.

Below are the principal tools and equipment. They are all easily available. More sophisticated items can only be bought from a floral supplier.

FLORAL FOAM

Probably the most useful floral mechanic, or support, especially for dry displays.

There are two distinct types: the green, soft foam for fresh flowers. This has to be soaked in water first. The greyish brown dry floral foam is used for dried arrangements.

Both types of foam come in a range of shapes and sizes: spheres, cones, bricks and tablets, but foam is easy to cut to any shape you want.

The common trade name is Oasis, and most florists call it by this.

WIRE MESH

Plastic coated wire mesh is the other main floral mechanic. You can use ordinary chicken wire, but this usually has to be purchased in larger quantities. It's also more scratchy inside the container and on your hands.

The mesh can be crumpled and squeezed into any shape container; although it can't be used in glass as it will be seen. Unlike foam, mesh can be re-used.

Mesh is sometimes wrapped around wet floral foam to prevent it from disintegrating.

OTHER MECHANICS

Metal pinholders are heavy discs covered in spines. These metallic hedgehogs are used in shallow containers. The flower stems are impaled on to the spines.

Plastic pinholders are for securing floral foam to a base with some other fixative like floral clay.

SCISSORS AND SECATEURS

Good sharp gardening scissors are really worth the investment. So are secateurs. Buy the best you can afford; they'll last much longer. Wirecutters are useful, but not vital, as strong scissors will cut through most wire, even mesh.

KNIVES

A sharp knife is useful for slicing woody stems and stripping foliage. For cutting floral foam, you'll find an ordinary old dinner knife is perfectly suitable; it doesn't need to be sharp, although it helps if the blade is long.

WIRE

There are various types of floral wire.

Stub wire comes in various cut lengths and different thicknesses (or gauges). Medium gauge wire is useful for virtually every technique, unless you're dealing with very heavy material.

Reel wire is handy for binding several stems together. Silver rose wire is similar to reel wire but is even finer.

TAPE

Gutta percha is a rubber-based, stretchy tape used for binding stems together or covering ones already bound with fine wire. It's available in shades of green as well as brown and white.

Floral adhesive tape is used for sticking floral foam together or to a container.

Double-sided tape and ordinary sticky tape can be handy for dried flower displays.

Tips and techniques

Every arrangement, from the simplest to the most complex, can benefit from a little knowledge about the plants themselves and how best to handle them.

CONDITIONING

Fresh flowers will last much longer if they are conditioned first. Conditioning enables the flowers to absorb maximum water to keep their heads upright and their petals firm and strong.

By cutting the stem end or, in the case of wooden stems, hammering them, the plant is given the opportunity to absorb as much water as possible. Some plants though need a little more help and this is explained below.

Strip and trim

Strip all lower leaves from the stems, as these will rot quickly underwater and become smelly. Now trim the stem ends at an angle. These two things done, give the plants a long drink.

Woody stems

Some plants, like chrysanthemums, roses and lilac have tough, woody stems which do not so readily draw up water when cut. To remedy this, split the base of the stem upwards with a sharp knife or crush the ends of the stem with a hammer or scissor handles. Immediately immerse into deep water.

Boiling water

Plants such as ranunculus and anemones need to be dipped into about 2.5cm (1in) of boiling water before being placed into cool water for a long drink. Protect delicate flowerheads from the steam by wrapping them carefully in kitchen paper towel.

Searing

Euphorbia, poinsettia and poppies all emit a milky substance which can be irritating to the hands. To stop this, singe the stem end with a lighted match before immersing the plant into cool water.

Hollow stems
Plants like dahlias and delphiniums have long hollow stems. For the water to reach the flowerhead, it's best to tip the plant upside down, fill the stem with water using a small jug, then plug the end with some cotton wool.

AFTER CONDITIONING
Once you've conditioned the flowers, add some flower food or conditioner to the water. You can buy this in small sachets, but it's just as easy to make you own by mixing fizzy lemonade with water (about 1:2) and a dash of bleach. Alternatively, use sugar or an aspirin.

RE-CONDITIONING
Even when conditioned and supplied with ample water, some flowers can still droop. When this happens, trim 2.5cm (1in) off the stem ends and place them in hot water for at least ten minutes.

When tulip heads droop, push a pin just beneath the flowerhead to disperse any trapped air bubbles; alternatively, carbonated water often does the trick and perks up weary looking blooms.

CONDITIONING FOLIAGE
To prolong the life of shrubs and woody stemmed foliage, you will need to hammer the stem ends well. You can also split the stem ends upwards to aid water absorption. Plants like ivy, hydrangea and heather like to be totally immersed in cool water before arranging.

Before you arrange any foliage, always strip off the lower leaves. Even waxy foliage will cause the water to discolour if left.

FLORAL FOAM
If you're using floral foam to arrange your flowers, make sure you soak the foam well first. Running the foam quickly under some water though isn't sufficient;

instead, leave the foam to soak in a small basin of water before you use it.

Flowers arranged in foam will need misting. And don't let the foam dry out.

Use floral adhesive tape for securing pieces of floral foam together and to your container. It works on wet and dry foam.

WIRING
To support the fragile stems of some dried flowers and to attach ribbon or other items into a dried flower arrangement, you may need to use florists' stub wire.

Since the arrival of the hot glue gun, many florists and flower arrangers avoid wiring where possible and glue things together. Although glue is an obvious advantage to many dried flower displays, some items are quickly put into place with wire (see double bows, below).

Strawflower heads dry beautifully, but their stems are very fragile. Before the flowers are fully dry, you'll need to insert a length of medium-gauge stub wire. Use a 7.5cm (3in) piece of wire and bend one end into a hairpin shape as shown opposite. Push the longer end in through the centre of the flower; pull it out the other side, in doing so the hairpin bend will pass through the flowerhead, leaving two wire tails. Twist these together to form the new 'stem'. This wire stem is now sturdy enough to be inserted into any arrangement.

Skewering

Use a wooden skewer or cocktail stick to secure fruit into an arrangement. Push the pointed end of the skewer into the fruit and the other end into the foam.

Making clusters

Create little clusters of flowers with gutta percha tape. This stretchy tape binds tightly round the flower stems, holding them without damaging them in any way.

Wiring bows

Create two or three ribbon loops and bind them at the base with wire. Twist the wire 'tails' together to make a 'stem'.

Once it has been wired, tease the ribbon loops out to create a full bow.

Paint spraying

Spray seedheads in a well-ventilated area, or even outside. Use newspaper to catch the excess paint mist.

All about drying flowers

Although many florists now stock a wide variety of dried material, it is extremely rewarding to dry some of your own.

Most garden plants can be dried with little skill or expense; as you become proficient, you can turn your hand to more taxing materials and methods.

There are three principal ways to preserve flowers and foliage: by air, with drying agents (dessicants) and with glycerine.

The key to drying any plant successfully is to pick or buy flowers and leaves in their prime. Wilting, fading or dying blooms will look as dismal dried as they did before.

If you are picking your own garden flowers, gather them on a dry day, preferably around noon when the plant is well nourished. Select flowers just before they reach full bloom, as they'll begin to open up when you dry them.

The same goes for bought flowers. Check they're bright, young blooms and don't be tempted to arrange them first of all. Dry them while they are at their best.

COLOUR
As the flowerhead dries, it will change colour, losing its brightness and acquiring a softer hue. This is, of course, the enchanting quality of dried flowers.

Like flowers themselves, some colours seem to endure better than others. Experiment with different types. Red seems to dry successfully, but certain yellows and pink can look dirty; although mustard yellow stays quite true. Blue doesn't seem to hold its colour very well.

It will also depend upon which method you are using. Drying with dessicants seems to retain a brighter and truer colour than air drying. Preserving foliage with glycerine most definitely changes the colour of the leaves; usually to a rich bronze tone. Different colours can be achieved using car antifreeze instead of glycerine (this is quite hazardous, though, see below).

AIR DRYING
The easiest method and one which is used most frequently.

Plants are usually hung upside down in a dull, airy place until they have dried out. They can be tied in small bunches or hung singly. As the stems shrink when they dry, use rubber bands which will contract with the plant.

Make sure the flowerheads get plenty of air circulating around them; turn them occasionally if necessary. It's also important that they are well out of direct sunlight, as this will fade them.

Some flowers prefer to be stood upright in a jar or piece of foam; teasels, onion seedheads and pompon chrysanthemums, for example. Hydrangea, gypsophila and bells of Ireland need to be stood in a container with a little water (about 2.5cm (1in)). Don't top up the water once it has evaporated; leave the plant to stand in the container until it is thoroughly dry.

Suitable plants include: strawflowers, hydrangeas, statice, sea lavender, roses, lavender, globe artichokes, gypsophila, golden rod, hops, larkspur, peonies, wheat, cornflowers, tansy flowers, onion heads, poppy seedheads, love-in-a-mist seedheads, sunflowers, Queen Anne's lace.

PRESERVING WITH DESSICANTS
This is the most time-consuming of the three methods, but the final results are excellent, making it well worthwhile. Flowers preserved this way should retain a brighter colour and crisper form. It's also the only way to preserve really delicate flowers like freesia, narcissi and helebores.

The most common drying agent is silica gel, which is sold by chemists as blue or white crystals. The crystals absorb the moisture from the plant.

The blue indicator crystals are simple to use as they turn pink when they draw up moisture.

Cover the bottom of an airtight container with the crystals and carefully lay the flowers on top (daisy types face down; others stem down). Very gently spoon more crystals over the flowers. Heavy-handedness at this stage can result in broken or damaged petals, so take care.

Now fix the lid on firmly and leave the crystals to work. This can take anything from one to four days. Check the flowers occasionally; when ready the petals should feel like tissue.

Suitable plants include: asters, narcissi, daisy chrysanthemums, freesias, roses, forget-me-nots, delphiniums, marigolds, peonies, pansies, violets, lily of the valley, gladioli, fuchsias, gerbera, tulips, verbena, lilies.

OTHER DESSICANTS

Borax is another dessicant to consider. It's cheaper than silica gel, but takes longer to work.

You'll need to mix the borax with dry silver sand (3:2). Drying flowers with a borax mixture takes up to two weeks.

USING A MICROWAVE OVEN

This whole process can be speeded up with the aid of a microwave oven.

Use a non-metallic container, without a lid, and pack the silica gel and flowers as before. Put them into the microwave oven, uncovered, together with a glass of water. Set the oven to high power and cook the flowers for one to four minutes. Delicate blooms will take less time than stronger, multi-petalled varieties.

PRESERVING WITH GLYCERINE

This method is reserved for foliage. Unlike other preserved material, glycerined foliage will be leathery and pliable. You can even wipe it with a damp cloth, and it should last almost indefinitely.

Instead of being dried out, the stems and leaves are encouraged to drink a glycerine solution. Gradually, this solution will replace the water in the leaves, making them supple and glossy and turning them a rich bronze colour.

Pick the foliage in early or midsummer; any later and the natural effects of autumn will be taking place, denying the leaves of water.

Mix up one part glycerine to two parts very hot water. Pour a little into a tall container. Now hammer the stem ends well and stand them in the glycerine solution.

The complete process will take up to four weeks. Check every few days and wipe any beads of glycerine 'sweat' from the leaves.

If the plant doesn't appear to be absorbing the glycerine, trim off the stem end and repeat the procedure.

Suitable plants include: most foliage, especially beech, oak, bracken, laurel, willow, box, magnolia, hawthorn, eucalyptus and rowan.

USING CAR ANTIFREEZE

Ethylene glycol, contained in car antifreeze, is a cheaper – although more hazardous – alternative to glycerine. As antifreeze comes in a range of colours, these will transfer themselves to the leaves, creating some interesting tones.

As antifreeze is poisonous and highly corrosive, use gloves to prepare the mixture (1:2 as above) and stand the foliage in plastic containers. The antifreeze will be absorbed in the same way as glycerine.

A guide to popular flowers

Note

The plants are listed by their common names; the Latin botanical name appears in italics. Some plants, like hydrangea, are commonly known by their Latin names.

PLANT	CONDITIONING	USES
Alstroemeria *Alstroemeria sp.*	Trim off stem ends; put in shallow water.	Good as a cut flower, although petals are delicate.
Anemone *Anemone sp.*	Cut the stem ends; dip into 2.5cm (1in) of boiling water for a few seconds. Give a long drink.	Good cut flower with interesting colour range. Unsuitable for drying.
Bird of paradise *Strelitzia regina*	Cut stem at a slant and put in a bucket of deep water.	Flamboyant although expensive flower.
Carnation *Dianthus sp.*	Cut stems between joints, put in shallow, tepid water.	Wonderfully long-lasting as a cut flower. Can be preserved with dessicants.
Chrysanthemum *Chrysanthemum sp.*	Crush stem ends, give long, cool drink. Foliage smells very unpleasant if left under water; so ensure leaves are stripped off.	Another long-lasting flower when cut; some varieties can be preserved with dessicants.
Cornflower *Centaurea dealbata*	Trim off stem ends and put in water.	Wonderful for country-style, fresh displays.
Daffodil *Narcissus sp.*	Trim stem ends, put in cool, shallow water. Keep away from other flowers while conditioning as stems emit toxic substance.	Quite long-lasting, inexpensive fresh flowers for spring arrangements.
Dahlia *Dahlia sp.*	Trim stems ends and put in water. For large specimens, turn upside down, fill with water and plug end with a little cotton wool.	Fabulous, multi-petalled blooms in rich colours for fresh displays. Some varieties can be preserved with dessicants.
Delphinium *Delphinium sp.*	Stems need plugging, see dahlia.	Lofty blue and mauve flowers. Can be air dried or with dessicants.
Forget me not *Myosotis sylvatica*	Not necessary.	Pretty sky blue, pink or white flower on flimsy stem. Can last well.

Freesia *Freesia sp.*	Trim stem ends and place in shallow, cool water.	Heavily fragranced flowers traditionally used at weddings. Can be preserved with dessicants.
Gerbera *Gerbera sp.*	Trim stems on slant, dip for a few seconds in boiling water, then give a long drink.	Large daisies in vibrant colours for fresh displays. Not suitable for preservation.
Gladiola *Gladiola sp.*	Cut stem ends and put in cool, shallow water.	Tall stems of opulent flowers in oranges, reds, yellow and white. Nip out end buds to encourage other flowers to open.
Gypsophila *Gypsophila paniculata*	Not really necessary.	Sprays of tiny white flowers look good with roses. Dries easily by air.
Iris *Iris sp.*	Trim stems on the slant and give a long drink.	Long stems with flag type flowers in deep blue, purple and yellow. Not very long lasting but an attractive fresh flower.
Lily *Lilium sp.*	Split the stems upwards and place in cold water.	Huge variety of hybrids with fabulous stamens. In white, pink and orange or bicolours. Many with flecks and spots.
Love-in-a-mist *Nigella damascena*	Little conditioning needed.	Papery blue flowers on stems with feathery foliage. Seedheads dry easily by air method.
Peony *Paeonia sp.*	Likes warm water after stem ends have been cut.	Pink and red, multi-petalled blooms. Dries by air or with dessicants.
Poppy *Papaver sp.*	Stems ends need searing with a flame until the tip goes black.	Papery red flowers. Cultivated varieties last better than wild ones. Their spectacular seedheads dry easily by air.

Rosa *Rosa sp.*	Garden roses need their stem ends dipped in boiling water before being given a long drink. Florists' roses need their ends hammered before receiving a long drink. Drooping roses can sometimes be revived with a little sugar in warm water.	Everyone's favourite! Long-lasting if properly conditioned. Also easy to dry by air or with dessicants. They preserve very well with the aid of a microwave oven.
Scabious *Scabiosa sp.*	These benefit from a really long drink.	Papery blue or white flowers make lasting fresh displays. Can be dried, if careful, with dessicants. (Also known as pincushion flowers.)
Sea lavender *Limonium tataricum*	This needs little conditioning as the plant looks virtually the same dry as when fresh. In fact stems can begin to rot if left too long underwater.	Used mainly as a dried flower. Dries where it is by air.
Statice *Limonium sinuatum*	Crush stem ends, although treat as sea lavender.	Grows easily in the garden in a range of bright colours. Very easy to air dry.
Stock *Matthiola sp.*	Crush stem ends well and strip all lower leaves which smell horribly if left underwater.	Strongly scented flowers which display well, even though they are not very long-lasting. In white, pink and shades of mauve.
Strawflower *Helichrysum sp.*	Give a drink in shallow water.	Brightly coloured flowerheads dry beautifully simply by hanging them upside down. Stems are fragile, so may need wiring before fully dry.
Sunflower *Helianthus annuus*	Cut ends and give really deep drink. Can be revived by lying whole plant in a bath of tepid water.	Giant, nodding heads are easily dried by hanging upside down.

Sweet pea *Lathyrus odoratus*	Trim ends of stems and place in deep, cool water.	Lovely summer flowers with heady scent. Fragile petals, so avoid handling. Will last reasonably well when cut. Available in a wide range of colours, so an excellent bloom for fresh arrangements.
Tulip *Tulipa sp.*	Trim stems at a slant and give a shallow, cool drink. Drooping heads can be revived with soda water or by stem with pin just under the flower.	Goblet shaped flowers in wide colour range. Spring flowers last well when cut as they continue to grow. Hothouse varieties are not so long-lived.

US GLOSSARY

PLANT NAMES

	UK	US
Asparagus meyerii	asparagus fern	fern asparagus
Aster movae-angliae	Michaelmas daisy	aster
Codiaeum variegatum	Joseph's coat	copton, cooperleaf
Eremurus	foxtail lilies	desert-candles
Ficus benjamina	weeping fig	Benjamin fig; Java fig
Gypsophila	gypsophila	baby's breath
Limonium sinuatum	yellow statice	notch-leaf sea-lavender
Limonium tataricum	white statice	tatariam sea-lavender
Monstera deliciosa	Swiss cheese plant	Mexican breadfruit
Ranunculus asiaticus	Ranunculus	Persian buttercup
Ricinus communis	castor oil plant	castor-bean
Solidaster x luteus	golden rod	goldenrod

USEFUL TERMS

UK	US	UK	US
chemist	drug store	kitchen paper	paper towels
cling film	plastic wrap	muslin	cheesecloth
cocktail sticks	toothpicks	panel pins	brads
craft plaster	plaster of Paris	petrol	gasoline
drawing pins	thumb tacks	plaited	braided
emulsion paint	latex paint	PVA medium	white or yellow glue
glycerine	glycerin	sticky tape	Scotch tape
grey	gray	vine leaves	grape leaves
jug	pitcher	wardrobe	closet
kitchen dresser	Welsh cupboard		

Index

Acknowledgements

The authors would like to thank the following people and companies who lent their support, merchandise and – in some cases – premises.

Clifton Nurseries Ltd, Clifton Villas, Warwick Avenue, London W9 for letting us photograph among their wonderful arbours and conservatories and for lending us a variety of beautiful plants, candle holders and containers.

Amy Louise Floral Design, High Street, Epping, Essex for keeping us supplied with a huge selection of flowers and containers.

Snapdragon Ltd, 268 Lee High Road, Lewisham, London SE13 for their fabulous pots, urns and other containers.

Bernard Thorp, 53 Chelsea Manor Street, London SW3 for an exquisite selection of printed fabrics.

Corbel & Claw, Victoria Park Road, London E9 for the Edwardian washstand on page 12.

Albert Smith of Hornchurch, Essex for supplying us with the two copies in oils of Van Gogh's Sunflowers on page 60 and the Cezanne still life on page 15.

Susan Williams for various props, homemade bread and other goodies.

Pauline Butler for the iron candle holder on page 32.

Geoffrey Drayton, High Street, Epping, Essex for supplying us with the beautiful Oriental screen on page 97.

My Fair Lady, 58 Exmouth Market, London EC1 for the copper pot featured on page 64.

Stitches & Daughters, 5–7 Tranquil Vale, Blackheath, London SE3 for loaning a selection of shiny silver candleholders and vases.

Lathams Country Store, High Street, Epping, Essex for the delightful pine shelves on page 98.

Al's Diner, Exmouth Market, London EC1 for essential supplies of food and drink.